The Euro Capital Market

The Euro Capital Market

DANIEL GROS and KAREL LANNOO

JOHN WILEY & SONS, LTD

Chichester · New York · Weinheim · Brisbane · Singapore · Toronto

Other Wiley Editorial Offices

John Wiley & Sons, Inc., 605 Third Avenue,
New York, NY 10158–0012, USA

WILEY-VCH Verlag GmbH, Pappelallee 3,
D-69469 Weinheim, Germany

Jacaranda Wiley Ltd, 33 Park Road, Milton,
Queensland 4064, Australia

John Wiley & Sons (Asia) Pte Ltd, 2 Clementi Loop #2–01,
Jin Xing Distripark, Singapore 129809

John Wiley & Sons (Canada) Ltd, 22 Worcester Road,
Rexdale, Ontaria M9W 1L1, Canada

HG 5422
.G68
2000

Library of Congress Cataloging-in-Publication Data

Gros, Daniel, 1955–
    The Euro capital market / Daniel Gros and Karel Lannoo.
        p. cm.
    Includes bibliographical references and index.
    ISBN 0-471-99762-5
    1. Capital market—European Union countries.
    2. Monetary policy—European Union countries.
    3. European Monetary System (Organization) I. Lannoo, Karel. II. Title.
HG5422G68 1999
332'.0414—dc21   99-32598
                                                  CIP

British Library Cataloguing in Publication Data

A catalogue record for this book is available from the British Library

ISBN 0-471-99762-5

Typeset in 11/13 pt Palatino by Wyvern 21 Ltd, Bristol
Printed and bound in Great Britain by Biddles Ltd, Guildford and King's Lynn.

This book is printed on acid-free paper responsibly manufactured from sustainable forestry, in which at least two trees are planted for each one used for paper production.

Contents

List of Tables

List of Graphs

Preface

This book builds upon the report of a Centre for European Policy Studies (CEPS) working party chaired by Tommaso Padoa-Schioppa on the implications of monetary union for Europe's capital markets. This project was launched in July 1997 and the recommendations, published in June 1998, contributed to the drafting of the European Commission submission on 'Financial Services: A Framework for Action' to the Vienna European Council (December 1998).

The book continues the work undertaken by CEPS since the mid-80s on European monetary and financial market integration, which has resulted in many articles, papers and books, the most well known being the standard work *European Monetary Integration*, by Daniel Gros and Niels Thygesen. Our aim is to rectify the lack of reference works on European capital markets. While working on the book, we were surprised to see that no unified and comprehensive treatment of this subject was available.

We are indebted to many persons who have stimulated our work and helped us with comments and advice, in particular Tommaso Padoa-Schioppa and our colleagues at CEPS. The members of the 1997–98 CEPS working party on 'Capital Markets and EMU' contributed to our first report on this subject. Special thanks go to Nuria Diez Guardia for research assistance and Isabelle Tenaerts for secretarial support.

Foreword

European Monetary Union (EMU) will lead to a truly unified capital market where once many individual markets had been kept separate by their national currencies. In spite of growing trade integration and the formal creation of a 'single market' for banking and financial services in 1992, currency segmentation had preserved strong differences in instruments, intermediaries and regulatory arrangements. The introduction of the euro thus constitutes a regime shift, which pervades the very structure of markets and the fundamental attitudes of operators. As such, it will force profound changes.

Our understanding of the depth of this transformation has just begun and requires a special intellectual effort. This book gives a valuable and timely contribution to this end. It documents the diversity and fragmentation of capital markets in Europe before the arrival of the euro. It shows that the euro has produced immediate changes in such areas as the foreign exchange and short-term markets, but it also analyses the transformation that has been set into motion in other areas, such as the longer-term capital markets.

EMU has come at a moment of profound change in the financial industry. Restructuring production and distribution lines, consolidating the large institutions into even larger ones, and breaking the frontiers of specialisation proceed at an accelerating pace under the pressure of increased competition and innovation. In 1998 banking was the most merger-intensive industry both in Europe and in the United States. A similar fever has gripped organised markets, although plans to connect European bourses and to link-up derivative exchanges do seem harder to implement than to conceive. Developments in telecommunications technology, especially the Internet, constitute a potential threat not only for the traditional equity markets, but also for mainstream financial services.

An interesting and intriguing aspect of the advent of the euro is that it constitutes at the same time an additional challenge and an opportunity to meet more effectively the pre-existing challenges. An additional challenge, because it suddenly broadens the size of the market in which institutions have to position themselves. An opportunity because, by adding to the very intensity of the overall challenge, it helps overcome the deep-seated resistance to change. Institutions and organised markets, often accustomed to a comfortable condition of public ownership and to a protected environment, are suddenly confronted with pressures and threats that can neither be ignored nor delayed.

The combined impact of the advent of the euro and the other factors of change poses new challenges not only to the market side, but also to the policy side of the financial system. The institutional framework to control and supervise markets and institutions comes under scrutiny to assess its fitness to the new reality and its likely change. Indeed, a more integrated market calls for a common regulatory and supervisory framework as well. How can this challenge be met? The search for adequate solutions will take time and will lead to arrangements that are hard to predict today. We can safely say, however, that to be both effective and politically acceptable, the search for solutions will have to resist the temptation of protectionism.

National champions, be they banks, financial conglomerates or organised markets, will only be successful if they are truly competitive in terms of both products and costs. The public interest to be pursued is no longer purely national, but has expanded in parallel with the enlargement of the market. Recognising this change is not an act of altruism, but rather a form of enlightened self-interest. Indeed, only this recognition will permit the avoidance of counterproductive decisions.

Some structures for supervisory co-operation already exist at the European level, as a result of EU legislative provisions (like the Banking Advisory Committee) or of voluntary initiatives of national agencies (like the Banking Supervision Committee, or Fesco, the forum regrouping Securities Commissions). Looking at the challenges ahead, it seems clear that these structures need to be streamlined, strengthened and perhaps reformed. Other fora may have to be created. Supervisors will also need to work closely, to the point of acting as a single collective body when needed.

The range of issues raised by the concomitant events of the transformation of the financial system that is happening at the global level, and the specific and strong additional factor of change provided by the euro, is wide. It includes the different segments of the industry. It covers both the market and the policy side of the system. It also spans technical as well as economic problems. The authors of this book have explored in a careful and competent way many facets of this complex problem.

This book is the first publication on the subject since the launch of the euro. It is a precious contribution to a debate on the structural implications of EMU and its consequences for policy and governance. I am convinced it will remain a useful reference in this debate.

Dr. Tommaso Padoa-Schioppa
Member of the Executive Board
European Central Bank, Frankfurt AM

Executive Summary

Capital markets, where debt and equity instruments are traded, have experienced huge transformations over the last quarter of the twentieth century. Markets have grown in size, depth and complexity, to a point where a single problem can have ramifications in different directions all over the globe.

The physical location of the market is becoming increasingly irrelevant. Markets are virtual and intangible. The grand stock exchange buildings which many capitals harbour have become empty shells, symbols of past times of the place where traders met and physically formed the market. Today, technological developments have replaced all that, and the market is formed by the screens placed in front of thousands of traders all over the world. The stock exchange buildings have at best been left with noisy machines which match trades, execute orders and disseminate information.

In contrast to the United States, banks are by far the most important intermediaries on the European market. Whereas in the US the financial system is fragmented as a result of historical and regulatory developments, Europe's capital markets are dominated by universal banks. The expectation that EMU will lead to a more market-based disintermediated financial system in Europe needs to be seen in this perspective.

So, why write a book about the euro capital market, if physical location is irrelevant, and markets are dominated by banks? Does the euro give a special aspect to capital markets based in Europe? Is the euro capital market so different from the dollar capital market that it deserves a special volume? We would answer in the affirmative. No true European capital market existed before EMU, only the euro has for the first time provided a specific European element in capital markets. The deeper and more liquid markets that will result from EMU should stimulate securitisation and, in the long run, tilt the euro capital market to a more market-based disintermediated financial system. This process raises a number of policy issues, related to the supervision of banks, the regulation of securities markets and the adequate taxation of savings.

WHERE DO WE COME FROM?

On the eve of EMU, Europe was characterised by a number of national markets that were interconnected via the foreign exchange markets. They were national in the sense that borrowers and investors tended to come from the same country and often used instruments specific to that country. Despite the single market programme, the regulatory framework is still a source of fragmentation, and household savings generally are not internationally diversified.

Most of the developments in Europe's national capital markets previously occurred as a result of a liberalisation *erga omnes*, allowing global developments to affect local markets. International integration has underscored the global dimension of markets, whereas EMU should lead to a concentration on the European dimension.

Marked differences can still be observed today in the structure of capital markets in the EU, both in terms of the instruments used and in the role and importance of financial intermediaries:

- Equity markets are very important in some countries, but underdeveloped in others.
- The importance of local bond markets depends on the size of the outstanding public debt and the instruments available for debt refinancing. Public debt is largely issued on the local market and is domestically held. Sizeable private bond markets exist in some countries, mostly in the Euro-bond and mortgage bond segments.
- Institutional investors are not internationally diversified. They have a strong preference for equity in some countries, but for government paper in others. Pension funds are major players in some countries but non-existent in others.
- The degree of bank restructuring differs in important respects across the EU. Bank profitability improved strongly in certain European countries in the first half of the 1990s, whereas it declined in others to reach worrying levels.

Capital markets tend to be either parochial (witness the home bias of households, the importance of local savings and loans, etc.) or global. There has been no European dimension so far. This should change with the euro.

THE IMPACT OF THE EURO

National markets were not unified immediately with the irrevocable fixing of exchange rates. Wholesale markets moved to the euro-quotation from day one of EMU, but the structural differences will not vanish overnight. EMU should nevertheless accelerate the process leading to an integrated European, and hence more liquid, mature and efficient capital market.

Some implications for the market are clear:

- A larger and more liquid bond market reduces the cost of funding debt both for governments and for the private sector. Spreads on sovereign bonds fell drastically in the perspective of EMU and are expected to remain within narrow bands for the euro-zone countries. Evidence of spreads and take-up in government bond markets in the first months of EMU confirms the advantage of a more liquid market for issuers. Corporate debt issues in euros have also seen a rapid take-off, although it is too early to say whether the current pace can be sustained. The structural differences to the US financial markets remain considerable.
- In organised markets, the effects are clearest in derivative markets. Derivative exchanges are linking up with one another or with the local stock exchange as they face the loss of business brought about by the disappearance of many foreign exchange and interest rate related contracts under EMU.
- In stock markets, the move to euro listing and the facility of remote membership will lead to a further reorientation of trades to a firm's domestic exchange, reducing the need for multiple listings within the EU and stimulating cooperation between exchanges. But the location of exchanges is becoming increasingly irrelevant as the technological revolution has anyway led to a situation where exchanges consist essentially of a network of computer links underpinned by common legal rules.
- EMU increases competition in the financial sector. Market integration as a result of EMU reduces concentration levels in banking at a *European* level, allowing further consolidation. Mergers and

acquisitions should, however, not be an end in themselves but a means to achieve better performance. EU bank profitability still has a long way to go and stands far below the levels noted in US banking.

Differences in national regulations and fiscal rules now constitute the main barrier to an integrated European financial market in EMU. For households, the cost of cross-border investment in terms of higher taxation and administrative requirements is likely to remain prohibitive. Institutional intermediaries can reduce the cost of administrative requirements, but they cannot change the fiscal rules, for example the fact that tax credits are often accorded only to residents.

The parameters for portfolio diversification changed with EMU. The introduction of the euro has eliminated currency-matching rules as a barrier to cross-border investment for insurance companies, but the elimination of currency risk might also reduce the benefits of cross-country diversification, since higher correlation between markets increases risk return. Credit risk should become more important in assessing the quality of sovereign issuers, but so far the market has not extracted high risk premia for differences in debt levels. However, the experience with state debt in the US or Canada also suggests that risk premia for sovereign debt should certainly be lower than the differentials observed before EMU. This should stimulate diversification into higher-yield non-sovereign securities.

That EMU will contribute to the development of a US-style capital market cannot be taken for granted. Structural differences between the two markets are deeply rooted and profound. The dominant role of banks in European capital markets will have a dampening effect on the rapid growth of securitisation and disintermediation in Europe. High levels of bank assets in Europe appear to be correlated with low levels of development of bond and equity markets, the opposite from the US situation. Also institutionalisation of savings in pension and investment funds is much less developed in Europe.

IMPLICATIONS FOR GOVERNANCE AND POLICY

The framework for supervision and regulation will have to evolve progressively to match the emergence of a European capital market. While monetary policy throughout the euro zone is run by a single institution, the European Central Bank (ECB), no provision has been made for the creation of common institutions to supervise the financial sector or to regulate capital markets. A truly integrated capital market will sooner or later call for a *common institutional framework* in this area as well. Although this does not necessarily imply that the euro zone requires a single supervisory authority, strengthened forums for cooperation between different national and European bodies are indispensable. Moreover, there is a need for *harmonisation cum deregulation*. European standards must in some cases be harmonised, but not necessarily increased to the level of the most restrictive member state.

The greatest need for improvement in the regulatory framework for financial services is in the area which is most changed by EMU, that is the securities markets. If securitisation is to develop as a result of EMU, authorities need to work to simplify issuing procedures, facilitate the work of intermediaries, and ensure common standards. A level playing field needs to be ensured for all intermediaries involved in the listing, trading, clearing, settlement and custody of securities.

Closer integration of securities markets also highlights imperfections in other elements of the regulatory framework. If issuing prospectuses are increasingly used on a cross-border basis, accounting standards, used in the underlying valuation, also need to be more harmonised. European authorities should thereby give maximum credit to International Accounting Standards to be accepted world-wide. Pressures for corporate governance systems to converge will also grow, but in that case, a market-driven approach is preferred to a top-down harmonisation. Corporate governance systems function within a specific economic and social context, which can in each case lead to adequate performance. Some guidance through a European-wide code of best practice might nevertheless be useful.

Since banks are the most important players on capital markets in Europe, banking supervision is also affected. As compared to securities markets, the regulatory framework for banking is more developed. The priorities that emerge relate to the optimal institutional structure for prudential control, the need for more coordination of supervision and the structure of cooperation with the European central bank. Since the ECB is only in charge of monetary policy, and financial stability and prudential supervision are kept at the local level, appropriate structures need to be put in place to ensure the stability of markets and allow adequate supervision of European banking groups. Since interpenetration of markets increases exponentially in EMU, financial stability problems could rapidly acquire European dimensions, with no single institution formally in charge. A three-pronged attack is necessary, involving greater cooperation between supervisory authorities, the creation of a European observatory for systemic risk, and alignment and control by the European Central Bank of lender-of-last-resort and bank exit policies at local level.

A final point of action concerns the taxation of savings income. Since the start of EMU, attention has focused on the proposed EU directive setting a 20% withholding tax on interest income obtained by EU residents in other member states. It should be clear, however, that this proposal touches only the tip of the iceberg. A truly integrated euro capital market will emerge if the other discrepancies in taxation documented in this volume are tackled as well. Much remains to be done in the areas of corporate income taxation, the treatment of dividends, capital gains, etc.

Introduction

Financial markets are special. Compared to industry, the financial sector is at one and the same time both more parochial and more global. It is more parochial in the sense that even large banks employ most of their personnel in their home country, whereas large industrial firms often employ as many people abroad as at home. European banks also do most of their business with, and earn most of their profits from, domestic customers, whereas foreign markets are even more important for many industrial enterprises than their domestic one. For example, most European car makers sell more vehicles abroad than in their home country.

Another indicator of the parochial nature of financial markets is the tendency of an overwhelming majority of households to exclusively use their domestic banking system. This contrasts sharply with consumption habits for consumer goods where most consumers are not even aware whether a product is produced domestically or is imported. A similar discrepancy exists in the allocation of assets by investors. It has long been observed in the academic literature that investors should diversify their holdings internationally because the returns from investments abroad are unlikely to correlate with domestic returns. A low degree of correlation among different assets means that investors would then be able to construct portfolios with a low overall risk, even if the foreign assets carried a larger absolute risk because of currency volatility. In practice, however, investors rarely take advantage of this possibility. Thus, one of the key questions for financial markets is whether investors will relinquish this home bias under EMU.

At the same time, however, financial markets are becoming more international since the impact of financial market shocks is often felt all over the world. As the recent crisis in Asia has shown, even local shocks can resonate in all corners of the globe within a matter of hours. This is not the case for other goods and services. If the market for cars dries up in any one country, consumers in another country will hardly notice.

There is another important characteristic of financial markets that sets them apart from other goods and services. The integration of goods markets is biased towards Europe. About two-thirds of the foreign trade of member countries takes place within the EU. The situation is different in financial services, but it is difficult to document since few systematic data exist on trade in financial services or on the magnitude of bilateral capital flows. The latest available data show that trade in financial services is much smaller than often believed. The total for the EU 15 (1995) was around ECU 15bn, which was only about 1% of all trade in goods. The total value-added of the financial services sector is estimated to be about ECU 300bn per annum. This implies that only about 5% of the value-added in this sector is traded, whereas up to 40–50% of output in industry is traded. Data on cross-border banking penetration confirm this situation of limited cross-border trade. In the five largest EU countries, only 4.25% of the assets and 6.2% of the liabilities were cross-border in 1996 (White 1998). Table I.1 provides some concrete examples of this phenomenon in well-known institutions. It shows that even the most international banks conduct most of their business at home.

This dual nature of their being both parochial and global makes it difficult to predict the impact of the introduction of the euro on European financial markets. We emphasise the formulation 'the introduction of the euro' because this is the really new element brought about by monetary union. The other elements of financial market integration were introduced some time ago: the abolition of capital controls dates from 1990, the second banking directive which established the internal

Box I.1 Global vs European Integration in Financial Markets

The importance of cross-border transactions for financial markets is extremely difficult to documenting. Data on trade in services have only recently been collected on a comparable basis and there is still no information on the size of credit and debit flows in financial services for one important country (the UK). Preference is therefore given to documenting the international integration of some important financial institutions that stand for different types, using one industrial firm, VW, for purposes of comparison. Table I.1 shows the distribution of some important elements (workforce, assets, profits or sales, depending on data availability) over three markets: domestic, rest of EU and rest of world.

Table I.1 How international are European banks with global ambitions?

	Domestic market (% share)	Rest of Europe (% share)	Rest of world (% share)
ABN-AMRO			
Employees	44.4		
Pre-tax profit	49.1	10.7	40.2
ING Group			
Employees	44.2		
Income	48.1	11.2	40.7
Pre-tax profit	71.4	10.3	18.3
Deutsche Bank			
Employees	64.5		
Assets	32.0	34.6	33.4
Income	62.9	19.6	17.5
For comparison			
Volkswagen			
Employees	52.2	23.3	24.6
Production (units)	37.7		
Sales (units)	23.4	34.9	41.8
Sales (income)	34.6	39.0	26.4

Source: Annual reports 1997 of the companies concerned.

It is interesting to note that the two financial institutions with a smaller home base have chosen to go global in the sense that the rest of the world accounts for a higher proportion of employees, assets or income than the rest of Europe. By contrast, Deutsche Bank seems on the way to becoming a European-oriented institution like VW, for whom Europe is more important than the rest of the world (although the recent acquisition of Bankers Trust might have changed this).

market in this sector came into force in 1993, followed by insurance and investment services in 1994 and 1996 respectively. However, we would expect that the introduction of the euro will lead to qualitative and structural changes in a way that the previous steps have not—at least for the core countries. The financial systems of some peripheral countries are still undergoing upheavals after having been for decades mostly government-owned and/or subject to heavy political intervention plus high and variable inflation rates.

A few direct consequences of the common currency could already be observed from 1 January 1999 onwards. There is a single money market interest rate; the interbank and foreign exchange markets are completely integrated; all foreign exchange derivatives based on the currencies of the participating countries have lost their *raison d'être*; and interest rates on government debt differ only to the extent that their perceived rating differs. There is more competition in banking. What more can we expect? How far will competition go in banking? Will it be limited to the wholesale market or will banks also start to compete for retail customers? Will equity markets become more integrated? Perhaps trading platforms will be integrated, but we have arrived at the conclusion that a host of national fiscal and regulatory differences will ensure that a German company remains different from, say, a French company, even if both are in the same sector and have a similar European-wide distribution of production and sales. Similarly, the share issues by these companies might also remain 'national' in the sense that investors will not be indifferent to the laws of the country in which a company is incorporated. For example, German investors are given a tax credit for corporate income tax paid by the company if it is German, but not if it is French. The reverse also holds: non-German investors in a German company do not receive the tax credit for German corporate income tax. These differences in corporate and personal income taxes plus the treatment of capital gains not only concern investors, but they also affect the financing structure of firms since they imply different optimal gearing ratios. Moreover, differences in corporate governance imply that similar companies might react quite differently to changes in business conditions (i.e. only a German company is governed by a two-tier board structure and is subject to *Mitbestimmung*).

Eventually, these differences will diminish as a result of tax and regulatory competition. It will take some time, however, for a single European, 'euro' financial market to emerge in the same way that a single dollar-denominated financial market exists in the US in which there are no regional differences in corporate financing structures or in investment patterns by households.

EMU comes at a time of rapid technological progress and continuing deregulation of financial markets in general. These processes do of course interact and are likely to accelerate the emergence of an integrated European financial market. But we concentrate on one aspect, namely the introduction of the euro as a catalyst for change.

This volume is organised as follows: Chapter 1 outlines the institutional and regulatory framework for the euro area and the single financial market: the European Central Bank's strategy and instruments, and the EU framework for capital market activities. Chapter 2 describes the different components of European capital markets on the eve of EMU and the intermediaries that are active in these markets. It examines the evolution that has taken place ahead of EMU and discusses country-specific characteristics. The implications of EMU for market restructuring are discussed in Chapter 3, which examines to what extent a more market-based system can be expected to emerge. Chapter 4 analyses the policy and governance issues that need to be addressed as a result of EMU. Statistical data and references to the regulatory framework are given in the Appendices.

1
The Institutional and Regulatory Framework

The first section of this chapter describes the institutional framework for the execution of common monetary policy in EMU, as laid down in the EU Treaty and by the European Central Bank (ECB). The second section discusses the regulatory framework for operators on capital markets in Europe, as it has been harmonised in the EU's single market programme.

THE EUROPEAN CENTRAL BANK
AND ITS MONETARY POLICY

The overriding goal of the common monetary policy is price stability. This goal has been enshrined in the Maastricht Treaty in very clear terms (see Box 1.1). The wording is clearer than that of the Bundesbank Act of 1957, which defines the main responsibility of the German central bank to be 'the safeguarding of the value of the currency' (Art. 3). Before the Maastricht Treaty, most other EU central banks operated under legal mandates that were even less clear with respect to the ordering of macro-economic objectives and more open to the imposition of the preferences of the government at any point in time. But this has now changed radically.

Box 1.1   Price Stability as the Primary Objective

Art. 2 of the European System of Central Banks (ESCB) Statutes states:

> In accordance with Article 105(1) of this Treaty, the primary objective of the ESCB shall be to maintain price stability. Without prejudice to the objective of price stability, it shall support the general economic policies in the Community with a view to contributing to the achievement of the objectives of the Community as laid down in Article 2 of this Treaty. The ESCB shall act in accordance with the principle of an open market economy with free competition, favouring an efficient allocation of resources, and in compliance with the principles set out in Article 3a of this Treaty.

This formulation is repeated in Art. 3a of the Maastricht Treaty.

It would be a mistake to look exclusively at legal texts to predict the future performance of the ESCB. Some national central banks whose statutory obligations place no special emphasis on price stability and whose political authorities enjoy little formal independence have nevertheless proved able to pursue such policies—for example through participation in the EMS. Yet it is significant that governments—and not just central banks—in the EU were prepared to subscribe to a clear and permanent, almost lexicographic ordering of their preferences with respect to the objectives of their joint monetary policy. Given the unanimity of central bankers on this point and the absence of any identifiable inflationary pressures at the moment, it is therefore likely that the European Central Bank will in fact be willing and able to pursue its assigned task. The choice of monetary policy targets and instruments has to be seen in this perspective as well, since they constitute the means by which the ECB can reach its aim of price stability.

The Institutional Framework

The institutional framework for monetary policy in the euro area is established in the Maastricht Treaty. Thus, we start by reviewing the relevant provisions in the Treaty. But to understand how the system works in reality one needs to go beyond the formal provisions and examine the balance of power between its different elements.

The Maastricht Treaty entrusts monetary policy to the European System of Central Banks (ESCB) which consists of a central institution, the European Central Bank (ECB), and the national central banks (NCBs). Formally all the 15 NCBs of EU member states are part of the ESCB. But in reality only NCBs from countries that have joined EMU (now 11) participate effectively, because only they participate in the decision-making organs. The subset of the ESCB that is part of the euro area is called the 'Eurosystem'. Since the participation of the non-euro countries in the ESCB is really only a formality, we will continue to use the term 'Eurosystem' synonymously with the term ESCB.

The head of the Eurosystem, the ECB, is located in Frankfurt and has two governing bodies: the Executive Board and the Governing Council. The Executive Board has six members, including the President and the Vice President. The Governing Council comprises the six members constituting the Executive Board and the governors of the eleven participating national central banks.

The Governing Council is vested with the main overall authority:

> The Governing Council shall formulate the monetary policy of the Community including, as appropriate, decisions relating to intermediate monetary objectives, key interest rates and the supply of reserves in the system, and shall establish the necessary guidelines for their implementation. (Art. 12.1 of the Statutes of the ESCB).

Implementation of policy decisions is left to the Executive Board:

> The Executive Board, shall implement monetary policy ... in-
> cluding by giving the necessary instructions to national central
> banks. (Art. 12.1)

Moreover, the Executive Board acts as the agenda setter, providing the structure to the meetings of the Governing Council. The Governing Council plans to meet at least once every two weeks, and more frequently if deemed necessary. This schedule suggests a close involvement of the Governing Council in all the phases of monetary policy-making.

Both organs can act on simple majorities and each member of the Governing Council has one vote.[1] This last provision is very important. The main argument against weighted voting was that it could have suggested that governors primarily represented national interests (as ministers do in the European Council) and were not equal members of a collegiate body charged with formulating a common policy for Europe. Acceptance of the one-man-one-vote principle must be seen as an important concession by Germany (and to a lesser extent by other large member states). It was obtained in return for the explicit mandate to preserve price stability and a high degree of independence for the ESCB. These were key conditions for obtaining Germany's assent to EMU. Together with assured long periods of tenure, and the role of the ECB Governing Council in future nominations to the Executive Board (the Governing Council has to be consulted before future nominations), the voting rule was supposed to assure that this decisive policy-making body would develop a high degree of cohesiveness and collegiality.

The principle that all members of the Governing Council have shed their nationality and share a common European vision is yet to be tested. In theory, the ESCB has to formulate the best monetary policy for Europe as a whole, disregarding national interests and points of view. In practice, the perspectives of national governors and Board members are likely to differ. The first nominations at the historic European Council of May 1998 caused intense political infighting at the highest levels because of the different nationalities involved. And so far, national central banks have struggled to retain as many competencies and as much freedom of manoeuvre in minor policy matters as possible.

The central element, the ECB, will certainly have a European (or rather euro area) perspective. Members of the Executive Board are likely to share a common view, based on daily collaboration and the same information sources. By contrast national central banks are more likely to retain national perspectives. Their governors are appointed through a national procedure, and generally by national politicians; their exposure to the media is primarily national. National central banks will feel they are accountable to national politicians and to a national public opinion. The governors will spend most of their time and efforts in their home country, dealing with national problems and addressing national audiences. It would be strange if these circumstances did not influence their thinking and their range of concerns. Moreover, whatever their incentives and their ultimate goals, representatives of national central banks will certainly absorb more local information, and less aggregate EU-wide information, than their ECB counterparts.

It is thus important to go beyond the Treaty's provisions to determine the real balance of power in the decision-making process within the Eurosystem. Who will carry most influence in the formulation of monetary policy: the ECB or the national central banks?

Number of Votes

Collectively, members of the Executive Board of the ECB have only 6 votes in the Governing Council, out of a total of 17 (a number that will rise as other countries join EMU). This minority position resembles that of the Bundesbank Board (*Direktorium*) prior to 1992, which numbered 7 (most of the time) on a Council (*Rat*) of 18 members (the other 11 were presidents of *Landeszentralbanken*). Germany is a single nation, however. Moreover, it has only one financial centre where the major money market participants are located and all foreign exchange operations take place. These factors strengthened the centre, despite the fact that discount quotas and operations were administered by the *Landeszentralbanken*. Nevertheless, even Germany felt the need to redress the balance when five new *Länder* joined. The 16 members representing the *Länder* were reduced to 9, thereby creating the current balance of 8:9 (for a total of 17).

In the United States, the Federal Open Market Committee (FOMC) has functions analogous to those of the ECB Governing Council: it sets monetary objectives and formulates guidelines for the main policy instrument—open market operations—to be undertaken through the Federal Reserve Bank of New York. FOMC meetings, held every five or six weeks, are attended by the 12 presidents of the regional Federal Reserve Banks and the 7 members of the Board of Governors. The latter are nominated by the President of the United States, subject to confirmation by the US Senate. Only 5 of the 12 Federal Reserve Bank presidents have the right to vote at any one meeting, however, and thus the majority lies with the Board—provided they agree, obviously. The central position of the Board is further underlined by the attribution to it alone of two important policy instruments: discount rate changes and variations in reserve requirements. Although these latter two instruments have recently lost their importance, the Board of Governors retains its dominant influence both on decisions and on implementation of policy, which is not difficult to supervise closely as it is done in one place, New York. This was not always the case. As analysed in Eichengreen (1992), the Federal Reserve was even less unified in its early years than the ESCB. The tentative and belated response of the Fed to the great depression was then also the main reason why its statutes were changed (Friedman and Schwartz 1963).

Personalities

A more subtle reason why one cannot compare the US Federal Reserve System to the ESCB solely on the basis of the numbers in their respective decision-making organs is that there is a huge difference in the type of personalities that represent the regional element. In the US, the presidents of the Federal Reserve District Banks are elected from among local shareholders, that is mostly commercial banks of the region. The presidents tend to be chosen for their managerial experience, rather than for their grasp of macro-economic issues or their reputation as defenders of price stability. Because of their background, even the district presidents who have the right to vote on the Board hesitate to take a strong position. They could find it difficult to engage in a sustained discussion on macro-economic issues with the members of the Federal Reserve Board and especially the President of the Fed, whose entire background might be concentrated in this area. A similar effect has operated in Germany, where a number of presidents of *Landeszentralbanken* had no prior experience in monetary matters or macro-economic policy and were nominated only on the basis of their local political connections.

Things are different in Europe. Some of the presidents of the NCBs have a strong background in macro-economic management and have had to take many more difficult monetary policy decisions than some members of the Executive Board. They are thus likely to voice their dissent. It is more difficult to predict the behaviour of the governors from the smaller countries that pegged their currencies to the DM, since they have not taken any significant policy decisions for decades. The presidents of NCBs from the smaller countries could determine the balance of power in the Governing Council depending on whether they side with the members of the Executive Board, or with their 'senior' colleagues from large neighbouring countries.

Staff

The experience of the Bundesbank and the Federal Reserve also suggests a third point. The strength of the centre is based on its superior back-up in terms of analysis and information. Even in federal countries, most of the staff preparing the background material for major monetary policy decisions are concentrated at the centre. This is different in the case of the ESCB. Table 1.1 shows the headquarters staff of a number of NCBs. The total staff of the ECB of some 500 is minuscule compared to the combined sum of some 60,000–70,000 at the component national central banks. Monetary policy is implemented by the latter, therefore they need more personnel. Even considering only the analytical staff (i.e. those not directly involved in the execution of monetary policy), however, it is clear that the ECB will not be an unquestioned authority: it will have to accept a number of national central banks from the euro zone as its equal.

The excess supply of personnel at the national level is one of the reasons why the ECB continues the practice adopted under the European Monetary Institute (EMI) regime, namely to have most important decisions prepared by committees drawn from the staffs of national central banks. These committees aim usually at reaching a consensus before a position is taken. Almost all such committees are currently chaired by an ECB staff member, which makes it more likely that the ECB is able to act as an agenda setter and exert a strong influence on the deliberations. Moreover, the ECB staff could have more aggregate, EU-wide, information than NCBs: national infor-

Table 1.1   *Headquarters staff at national central banks*

	Total staff	At headquarters	In analytical functions (research, statistics, economics, etc.)	Research
ECB		500	100–150	20–50
NCBs				
Germany	17,632	2,770	360	70
France	16,917		750	280
Italy	9,307	2,000	300	150
Spain	3,269		350	
Netherlands	1,721	1,500	165	60
US	23,727	1,700	350	

Source: Morgan Stanley, *Central Banking Directory* (1997), and national central banks; 1995 data.

mation is aggregated at the ECB, and analysed according to statistical and theoretical criteria chosen primarily by the ECB staff. Nevertheless, it is not always clear whether the ECB staff will feel more loyalty to the ECB or to a national central bank. The ECB has continued the staffing policy of the EMI by recruiting almost all of its staff through secondments from NCBs. As these secondments are usually limited in time, the ECB staff could retain their loyalty to their home NCBs and may not develop the *esprit de corps* that has characterised, for example, the Bundesbank and that has proven crucial when the institution is under pressure.

Finally, the imbalances in the staff numbers are not likely to be corrected any time soon, despite the recent decision to hire more staff at the ECB. Personnel issues have a direct bearing on the financial accounts of the ECB, and as such, are decided by the Governing Council without the Executive Board members and under weighted voting. Any attempt by the Executive Board to strengthen its personnel base would thus have to be approved by those who have the most to lose, namely the large NCBs. This situation is the opposite to that in the US, where the President of the Board of Governors in Washington must approve the budgets of the regional District Banks.

Differences among National Capital Markets and a Common Monetary Policy

Does it really matter if the monetary policy for the euro area is decided by a Governing Council in which the national elements dominate? The following quote from Friedman and Schwartz (1963: pp. 415–416) provides an eloquent description of the danger of entrusting monetary policy to a large and heterogeneous committee:

> A committee of twelve men, each regarding himself as an equal of all the others and each the chief administrator of an institution established to strengthen regional independence, could

much more easily agree on a policy of drift and inaction than on a co-ordinated policy involving the public assumption of responsibility for decisive and large-scale action. There is more than a little element of truth in the jocular description of a committee as a group of people, no one of whom knows what should be done, who jointly decide that nothing can be done. And this is especially likely to be true of a group like the Open Market Policy Conference, consisting of independent persons from widely separated cities, who share none of that common outlook on detailed problems or responsibilities which evolves in the course of long-time daily collaboration.

Friedman and Schwartz thus characterised the decision-making process of the Federal Reserve Board in the US in the 1930s. In Europe the committee in question would be the Governing Council of the European Central Bank and it already has 17 members, which could soon become over 30 when the Eastern enlargement of the EU is completed.

In the US context, the heterogeneity of backgrounds is stressed as one important cause of inefficient decision-making during the 1930s. History will not repeat itself, but the analysis of Friedman and Schwartz (1963) emphasises elements that are present in the Eurosystem as well. If the members of the Governing Council always had the same point of view, its size and composition would not matter. But there are several reasons why national considerations could play a role in the decisions of the Governing Council, no matter what the Treaty says. Differences among national capital markets play a role in each case.

Redistribution

A first reason for national voting patterns is that monetary policy can redistribute income between debtors and creditors. Countries with high public debts benefit from lower real interest rates, if such low rates can be delivered, because tax distortions are diminished. This obvious consideration lies at the heart of the fiscal convergence criteria and the requirement that central banks enjoy complete independence. As public debt ratios differ widely within Europe, this could remain an important source of disagreement between different national central banks. Central bank independence does not remove this disagreement, because it is really in the interest of the citizens of highly indebted countries, and not just of their governments, to have low real interest rates.

A related source of conflict between countries in the euro zone concerns the stability of the banking sector. Suppose that a banking crisis erupts in a specific country. The ideal monetary policy for that country could call for more expansion of credit, to prevent the spread of contagion effects to other sound banks. If the contagion is likely to spread to other countries in Euroland, this could become an important source of nationalistic conflicts. We address this important concern more extensively below.

Cyclical De-synchronisation

Even neglecting debtor–creditor relations, the evaluation of monetary policy could differ across countries in Euroland if they are at different stages of the business cycle. A good example is Ireland, which is currently growing much faster than the rest of the euro area, with signs of local overheating on the labour and the real estate markets. The Governor of the Irish Central Bank showed his preference for higher interest rates by keeping them several points above those of Germany for as long as possible. How likely is it that the same person should change track within a few weeks, and vote in favour of an interest rate cut to avoid deflation elsewhere in Europe?

The history of the federally organised national central banks suggests that regional considerations can play a role even within quite homogeneous political systems. The presidents of *Landeszentralbanken* in eastern Germany, where the state of industry is more depressed, were more inclined to favour low interest rates. The President of the *Landeszentralbank* of Hesse (which includes Frankfurt) was at times accused by his colleagues from other *Länder* of only being concerned with the large banks in 'his' Frankfurt, whereas they had to take into account the interests of the myriad smaller banks that dominate the banking scene in the provinces. It is difficult to verify whether this also happened systematically within the Federal Reserve System. The by-laws of the Fed forbid district presidents to vote on the basis of local interests. Thus, the motivations given for votes cannot be used to assess the intentions of the district presidents. The few systematic studies that have tried to relate the vote of district presidents to the state of the economy in their district have not reached strong conclusions.

Differences in Financial Structures and Monetary Transmission

There is yet another reason for nationalist voting, which interacts with the previous one: the impact of monetary policy differs across countries, because of differences in financial structures. Three broad angles of approach can be distinguished in the academic literature on the mechanisms used to transmit monetary policy. Some studies just document differences in financing patterns (see in particular, Borio 1995, but also Dornbusch, Favero and Giavazzi 1998). For example, in some countries, enterprises rely more on long-term capital (e.g. in Germany) than in others (e.g. Italy). Any move of the ECB that somehow twists the yield curve could then have differential national effects. For instance, an increase in short-term rates that reduces inflationary expectations and hence leads to lower long-term interest rates might have opposite effects on economic activity in Germany and Italy.

Other studies have relied on small VAR models to estimate the short-run impact of changing short-term interest rates (the main policy instrument of the ECB) on prices and demand (see Gerlach and Smets 1995). This approach is subject to the so-called Lucas critique in its severest form, however: past correlation cannot contain a lot of information here. For example, the central bank reaction functions must all change if only because there can no longer be a correlation between national variables and monetary policy. Moreover, the reaction function of the ECB will surely be different from that of a follower in the EMS or that of a central bank that has spent the last ten years in achieving convergence towards Germany.

A third way is to use existing small-scale models whose structural relations can be assumed to be less affected by EMU. A comparative study by the Bank for International Settlements (see Borio 1995) showed that there are differences in the timing and the strength of the transmission of monetary policy. France and Germany show in general a slower response than other countries. Somewhat surprisingly, the differences in the impact effects reported by Dornbusch, Favero and Giavazzi (1998) are actually small and statistically not significant, whereas the effect after two years is twice as strong for Italy than for Germany, France and Spain. One reassuring element of these studies is the fact that the Franco-German couple, which alone accounts for about half of the GDP of the EU 11 area, shows a very similar pattern.

Differences in financial structures, which are behind differences in the monetary policy transmission mechanism, are not exogenous to the monetary policy regime. But there has been little convergence in financing structures even in countries with essentially the same macro policies for a decade (Germany, France, Austria, Belgium, and the Netherlands). The main reason is that tax systems are more important for financing structures than inflation (as long as it remains moderate). Since EMU will not lead quickly to a harmonisation of taxes, this suggests that financial differences could last over a long time.

Implications: a Weak Centre in a Heterogeneous Area?

The ECB Executive Board is thus likely to be weaker than its German or US counterpart, with respect both to decision-making and policy implementation. The Board will be squeezed between the Governing Council, the repository of all policy-making authority, and the participating NCBs, which will be anxious to preserve as much influence as possible. The balance of power could rest much more with the national central banks than with the ECB itself. This need not be a disaster, however, as long as the NCBs abandon their national perspective and fully accept the task of formulating the best monetary policy for Euroland, based on a common vision and understanding. It is not clear yet whether this shared vision will develop. If it does not, the decision process will rely on consensus-building and compromises between individuals with a heterogeneous background, and different perspectives and information.

The most divisive issues within the Eurosystem have so far been all those decisions that bear on the potential of different countries to become financial centres. Divergences in this respect are likely to grow over time as money and other financial markets concentrate within the euro area. The voting power held by all those countries that are likely to lose their domestic financial centres might then become decisive.

Strategy

As regards the monetary strategy, the ECB's Governing Council opted for a combination of an inflation target for the longer-term framework and an intermediate monetary target. Three other possibilities were rejected: interest-rate pegging—because of well known theoretical objections to the stabilising properties of such a system; exchange-rate targeting—because the Treaty gives little emphasis to this objective (which is appropriate given that the euro area will be relatively closed); and nominal income targeting—inter alia because it would not relate directly to the goal of price stability. The dismissal of this third option is arguably a bit summary, but the two alternatives retained probably suffice to give the ECB the appropriate guidance.

Given the primary role of price stability in the Treaty's assignment of tasks to the ESCB, it is unavoidable that this objective will have to figure as an essential objective. The ECB provided a quantified definition of its ultimate objective, when it defined price stability as an increase in prices of less than 2%.

An inflation objective alone, however, is not enough: the time lag between a particular monetary policy action and its impact on inflation is simply too long to offer sufficient guidance for setting policy on a weekly basis. A first requirement for this strategy to work is for the ECB to develop and make publicly known its forecast of inflation for one to two years and to contrast it with its quantitative objective. Any discrepancy would constitute grounds for the use of monetary instruments, essentially interest rates.

Countries that have experience with inflation targeting, notably the United Kingdom within Europe, have found it useful to develop intermediate objectives which can help to assess the risks to price stability. At the insistence of the Bundesbank, which has had favourable experience with monetary aggregates and especially over the past decade with broad money (M3), the latter has been given the role of prime indicator of future inflation. But before it can become a useful intermediate objective it has to be demonstrated that its useful qualities carry over into the EMU period. The introduction of the euro is clearly equivalent to a major monetary reform that makes it uncertain whether the stability in the relationship of broad money to nominal income, as found in the part for the aggregate for the 11 EMU participants, will persist beyond 1999. While there are reasons to believe that money demand will become less stable after 1999, the relationship between past and future prices as well as the relationship between prices and the business cycle should not be much affected by the introduction of the euro. Hence, the initial emphasis is likely to gravitate towards the inflation-targeting mode.

The degree to which money demand will no longer be predictable in the first years of EMU is difficult to gauge. Some observers (e.g. Von Hagen 1997) have argued that the introduction of the euro should leave the money demand for transactions purposes unaffected whereas the demand for precautionary purposes (including savings deposits) might become more unstable as the evolution of interest and inflation rates becomes more uncertain. Most money is held by households, however, which might not take much notice of EMU until 2002. The transactions pattern of households is indeed likely to be unaffected by the introduction of the euro. The opposite could be argued for firms: their transactions and payments patterns might be strongly affected as international transactions play a much more important role for the corporate sector. Economies of scale in treasury that come with the single currency should lead to a significant reduction in the transactions demand by the corporate sector. Since the corporate sector holds about 30% of all transactions money, the impact on the overall narrow monetary aggregate M1 might be limited. The demand for cash, which is presumably used mainly by households, should be completely unaffected until 2002. For savings deposits, again held almost exclusively by households, it is difficult to predict what will happen. Why should the irrevocable fixing of exchange rates lead households to change their propensity to hold this type of asset rather than, say, money market accounts or bonds? The continuous evolution of technology and financial markets will of course have an impact on the demand for savings deposits, but these developments are independent of EMU.

All in all, it appears that the argument that EMU will make money demand unpredictable and that monetary targets will therefore become useless has been exaggerated. Households hold most of the money stock, whether narrow or wide, and their demand is unlikely to be affected by the introduction of the euro, at least until 2002. Moreover, the research by Monticelli and Papi (1996) suggests that the aggregate demand for money of the EMU area should be more stable than national money demands (including Germany's, which until 1999 constituted the anchor for the rest of Europe). The main argument for an explicit inflation target might be that the European public, which is not used to the implicit inflation target contained in the Bundesbank's monetary target, does expect one.

Monetary Instruments

The ESCB operational framework for monetary policy operations consists of open market operations, standing facilities and minimum reserves.

Open market operations, aimed at the provision or absorption of liquidity, consist of four main types, which differ in frequency and maturity, all of which can be either liquidity providing or absorbing.[2]

- Main refinancing operations: regular reverse transactions with a weekly frequency and a maturity of two weeks
- Longer-term refinancing operations: reverse transactions with a monthly frequency and a maturity of three months, intended to cater for a limited part of the total refinancing volume
- Fine-tuning operations: adapted to the prevailing circumstances and to the specific objectives of managing the liquidity situation in the market or of steering interest rates
- Structural operations: intended to affect the structural position of the banking system *vis-à-vis* the ESCB

Five types of instruments can be used for these operations—repurchase agreements or collateralised loans, outright purchases, issuance of ESCB debt certificates, foreign exchange swaps and collection of fixed term deposits—employed in combination with three different procedures (normal and quick tenders, and bilateral procedures).

As part of the standing facilities, the ECB provides and absorbs overnight liquidity at fixed rates. The marginal lending facility thus sets a ceiling and the deposit facility a floor for overnight rates.

Open market operations are executed by all the participating NCBs at the same time and under the same conditions. Bilateral operations are executed on a rotating basis by small groups of different NCBs. Standard tenders for refinancing operations are announced at the end of a business day ($t-1$), with a deadline for submissions at 9:30 a.m. the following day (t). Tender results are made public two hours later, with settlement following the day after ($t+1$). With quick tenders, this process happens over 2 hours. The ECB can either set a fixed rate or a fixed quantity. Monetary policy is executed through the ESCB's payment system TARGET (see Table 1.2).

A remunerated reserve requirement of 2% is applied on

Table 1.2 The monetary policy operations of the European System of Central Banks (ESCB)

Monetary policy operations	Types of transactions		Maturity	Frequency	Procedure
	Provision of liquidity	Absorption of liquidity			
OPEN MARKET OPERATIONS					
Main refinancing operations	• Reverse transactions	—	• Two weeks	• Weekly	• Standard tenders
Longer-term refinancing operations	• Reverse transactions	—	• Three months	• Monthly	• Standard tenders
Fine-tuning operations	• Reverse transactions	• Foreign exchange swaps	• Non-standardised	• Non-regular	• Quick tenders
	• Foreign exchange swaps	• Collection of fixed-term deposits			• Bilateral procedures
	• Outright purchases	• Outright sales	—	• Non-regular	• Bilateral procedures
Structural operations	• Reverse transactions	• Issuance of debt certificates	• Standardised/non-standardised	• Regular and non-regular	• Standard tenders
	• Outright purchases	• Outright sales	—	• Non-regular	• Bilateral procedures
STANDING FACILITIES					
The marginal lending facility	• Reverse transactions	—	• Overnight	• Access at the discretion of counterparties	
The deposit facility	—	• Deposits	• Overnight	• Access at the discretion of counterparties	

Source: European Central Bank, 1998.

deposits of banks and financial institutions which hold accounts with the ESCB. The reserve requirement applies to the following items of the liability base: overnight deposits; deposits with agreed maturity up to two years; deposits redeemable at notice up to two years; debt securities issued with agreed maturity up to two years; and money market paper. The holdings can be averaged over a certain period so that banks have some leeway in their liquidity management.[3]

Institutions subject to the reserve requirement are eligible for standing facilities and regular open market operations. Counterparties for monetary policy operations must be located in the euro area, and at least be subject to harmonised supervision at European Economic Area (EEA) level as further to the Second Banking Directive. At the end of the day, all debit positions of counterparties are automatically considered as a recourse to the marginal lending facility.

Lending by the ESCB (liquidity-providing operations) has to be based on adequate collateral (Art. 18 of the ESCB statutes). With the aim of protecting the ESCB from incurring losses in its monetary policy operations or in the provision of intraday credit in TARGET, ensuring the equal treatment of counterparties and enhancing operational efficiency, underlying assets have to fulfil certain criteria in order to be eligible for ESCB monetary policy operations. The list of eligible assets, first published by the ECB on 26 October 1998, is deemed by the ECB to fulfil these criteria.[4]

Eligible assets as collateral for ESCB credit operations are subdivided in two tiers. This does not imply a difference in the quality of the assets or their eligibility, but reflects differences in financial structures across the member states.

- Tier one consists of marketable debt instruments which fulfil uniform euro area-wide eligibility criteria specified by the ECB. The assets must be located in the euro area and denominated in euros, the issuer can be located in the European Economic Area (EEA) Norway, Iceland, Liechtenstein
- Tier two consists of additional assets, marketable and non-marketable (loans on the books of banks), which are of

particular importance for national financial markets and
banking systems and for which eligibility criteria are established by national central banks, based on minimum standards set by the ECB. The assets must also be located in
the euro area, denominated in euro, and the issuer needs
to be located in the euro area

No distinction is made between the two tiers with regard to
the quality of the assets and their eligibility for the various
types of ESCB monetary policy operations (with the exception
that tier two assets are not normally used by the ESCB in
outright transactions). At present, the list of eligible assets
contains around 19,000 tier one assets and around 1,800
marketable tier two assets. The outstanding value of marketable
assets amounts to around 5,000bn euro. Non-marketable tier
two assets are not included in the list on an asset-by-asset
basis. Both forms of assets can be used on a cross-border basis
within EMU, that is counterparties may obtain funds from the
national central bank of the member state in which they
are established by making use of assets located in another
member state. A correspondent central banking model, under
which central banks act as custodians for each other, is thereby
used.

Risk control measures are applied to collateralised assets. The
value of the underlying assets must be equal to the amount of
the credit granted plus a 2% initial margin, taking into account
the exposure time for the ECB. In addition, a valuation discount
(or 'haircut') of up to 5% is applied, according to the residual
maturity of the assets (with probably a larger haircut for tier
two assets).

All assets eligible to be used in monetary policy operations
can also be used to collateralise intraday credit in TARGET, the
ESCB real-time payment system. In addition, for the collate-
ralisation of intraday credit, TARGET participants may use
collateral proposed by EU national central banks of non-
participating member states; EU national central banks in participating member states can admit such collateral, but only for
the purpose of collateralising intraday credit. Such collateral
has the same quality standards as the assets eligible in the euro

area. These assets are not included in the list of eligible assets published by the ECB.

The list of eligible assets is updated on the Internet on a weekly basis. The updates will be made available to the public at 8 a.m. ECB time (CET) each Friday. In addition, the ECB reserves the right to exclude, at any time, individual assets from use in ESCB monetary policy operations. Procedures for monitoring and continuous checking have been put in place to ensure that the list remains up to date, accurate and consistent.

On the whole, the ESCB operational framework reflects what was in place in the different member states, with the exception of the discount window, used in Germany to provide liquidity at a preferential rate, which was abandoned. The standardisation of collateral should be an important incentive to market integration, but the decentralised execution of monetary policy might hamper it at the same time. Markets will continue to deal with the NCBs as their main contact with the system as it is the NCBs that will execute reverse and fine-tuning operations. They collect repossession ('repo') bids from local markets and send them to a central computer in Frankfurt, which allocates the repos according to the ECB's criteria, once all bids are collected and the market price is determined. The freedom given to NCBs on tier two assets could be used to protect the local market. Moreover, there is no remote access for financial institutions to other NCBs. Banks have to work through their own NCB, although this can be reviewed by the ECB.

THE REGULATORY FRAMEWORK FOR CAPITAL MARKET OPERATORS AND PRODUCTS

From a regulatory point of view, the single market for operators on capital markets is almost complete. With the exception of pension funds, EU markets have been opened up for the free provision of banking, investment and insurance services with a single licence. The liberalisation was implemented in different phases: in 1993 for banking, mid-1994 for insurance and 1996 for investment services. This applies also to foreign-owned institutions, which often enjoy a more favourable treatment in the EU than in their home market. This is, for example, the case for US financial institutions, which are constrained by Glass–Steagall-type barriers on universal banking at home. Expressed in GATS language (General Agreement on Trade in Services), the EU offers effective market access, which goes further than the national treatment provided in the World Trade Organisation (WTO) framework.

The same cannot be said for the regulatory framework for financial products. This applies mainly at retail level, but also at the wholesale level, or has implications for the latter. Differing regulations at retail level can hamper securitisation of products and thus affect the wholesale level. Apart from unit trusts, common rules for securities emissions, initial public offerings and stock exchange listings are much less developed. Although legislation is in place, harmonisation has gone insufficiently far and implementation leaves much to be desired to make mutual recognition work. The latter is related to the regulatory route followed in financial market integration in the EU, and in the single market programme (SMP) as a whole. Only essential rules are harmonised, the rest is subject to mutual recognition. Minimal harmonisation is done through *directives*, which are EU legal instruments which need to be transposed into national law by the member states. *Regulations* are instruments that are directly applicable in the member states, but they are less often used for market integration.[5]

The Regulatory Framework

In the single market programme, the financial services sector is divided along functional lines. Legislation is aimed at the three traditional components of the financial services sector: banking, securities brokerage and insurance. These activities are exercised in different legal entities in the member states. The first category comprises commercial banks, savings banks, mutual or cooperative banks, and mortgage banks or building societies. The legal status of the firm is used as a basis for including them within the scope of the directives on credit institutions.[6] For investment services, on the other hand, the services provided, which embrace a series of instruments, are used to define which firms are covered. This means brokerage, dealing, market-making, portfolio management, underwriting, investment advice and safekeeping of transferable securities, money market instruments, futures and options, and exchange- and interest-rate instruments.[7] In common terms, these are merchant or investment banks, securities firms, and stockbrokers and dealers (*agents de change*). Insurance comprises life and non-life insurance companies, defined as undertakings that have received an official authorisation to provide these services. They may be structured in different legal forms: plcs, mutuals or cooperatives, and federations.

These distinctions are to a certain extent arbitrary, however, and are not equally clear-cut for every member state. Above all the distinction between credit institutions and investment services poses problems. In Germany, for example, investment services are generally not separate legal entities and are therefore supervised along with banks ('universal banks'). In the United Kingdom, on the other hand, supervisory authorities preferred that the same entity does not transact both kinds of business under one roof. Instead, it was more common for securities business to be performed through a subsidiary with a separate legal status from the parent institution. Hence the directive of investment services had to take these national differences in institutional set-up into account. Significantly lower capital requirements for investment firms than for credit institutions would penalise countries with a universal banking structure. Therefore, universal banks can calculate the capital requirement for their trading books on the same basis as investment firms. Credit institutions, on the other hand, have to be regulated more rigorously because they are involved in deposit-taking.

Insurance and banking are still regulated as separate entities in all member states. Many financial institutions are, however, expanding the scope of their services and becoming financial conglomerates (*bancassurance* or *Allfinanz*), which creates new problems for supervisors. This is clearly the case in the banking sector, where many banks are already providing life and old-age insurance products through their distribution networks, with separate authorisations.

Four key directives define the provisions that had to be harmonised by the member states in order to allow free cross-border provision of services in each area: (i) the second banking directive; (ii) the investment services directive; (iii) the third life; and (iv) non-life insurance directives. Basically, these directives give financial institutions the opportunity to present their services across the EU with a single licence, after having duly notified their home authorities of their plans with regards to this or another market. The key measures are supplemented by one or more directives defining specific subjects, such as, for example, the own funds and solvency-ratios directives in banking and the capital adequacy directive for investment firms and trading departments of banks. The latter directives set the minimum capital standards for these firms. Harmonisation often extended to other areas that needed to be tackled at the European level to create the level playing field, for example, the directives on money laundering and insider trading. Table A2.1 (in Appendix 2) gives an overview of the EU regulatory framework for the financial services sector.[8]

The key issue in prudential control is the solvency of financial institutions. Such control should guarantee that these firms have a cushion with which to respond to sudden demands of clients or financial shocks. In banking, in accordance with the 1988 Basle Capital Accord (Box 1.2), a minimum solvency ratio of 8% is required, measured as the proportion of own funds of the risk-adjusted value of a bank's total assets and certain off-balance-sheet items. These rules are implemented for the EU in the solvency ratio and own funds directives.[9] In addition, deposit guarantee schemes are made obligatory in the EU. The large exposures directive requires banks to have a wide spread in their loans and prevents them from becoming too dependent on a few big clients.

Box 1.2　The Basle Capital Accord

The 1988 Basle Capital Accord, concluded by the G-10 Committee of Banking Supervisors, based in Basle, calls for a minimum 8% ratio of capital to risk-weighted credit exposure. At least half of the recognised capital must be in the form of core, or tier one capital, including common stock, non-cumulative preferred stock and disclosed reserves. The remainder, termed supplementary, or tier two capital, includes such components as undisclosed reserves, general loan-loss, provisions, asset-revaluation reserves, hybrid capital instruments and subordinate debt. The specific items recognised as tier two capital vary, however, and subordinate debt is limited by the Accord to 50% of tier two capital. General provisions can qualify as tier two capital only if they do not reflect a known deterioration in the value of assets.

Credit exposures are assigned to five broad categories of relative risk. They are given weights ranging from 0 to 100%. The most important ones are:

		Risk Weight (%)
1.	Loans to official OECD borrowers	0
2.	Claims on banks from OECD countries	20
3.	Inter-bank claims of less than one year	20
4.	Residential mortgages	50
5.	Foreign currency loans to non-OECD countries, all other credits to the private sector	100

According to the OECD, banks in European countries for which data are available have a solvency ratio well above 8%, with most countries having ratios of about 12% (see Table 1.3). It is interesting to note that there is no immediate relation between the profitability ratios, measured as return on assets, discussed below (see Table A1.6 in Appendix 1) and the solvency ratio. Countries with higher profitability ratios do not necessarily have higher solvency ratios, and vice versa. This underlines the relativity of the solvency ratio, or indicates that other elements affect the soundness of banks. The Banesto Bank in Spain went bust with a solvency ratio of 9%, but did not make sufficient provisions for bad loans. Japanese banks

Table 1.3. *Solvency ratios (1996) in banking*

B	13.7
DE	10.2
EL	10.4
E	12.3
F	9.8
I	12.9
NL	11.4
AU	13.8
P	11.1
SW	16.3
UK	11.5
USA	12.7
J	9.2
CH	10.3

Source: OECD (1998); data for France and Germany are approximations, based upon information from the largest banks; no data are available for other EU countries.

continue to have ratios above 8% but many of them are on the brink of bankruptcy. The need for reform and refinement of the Basle Ratios, currently under discussion, is thereby clear.

Solvency ratios for investment firms are set in the capital adequacy directive (CAD), but these rules are also applicable to the trading books of universal banks if these institutions choose not to subject their total business to the banks solvency ratios directive (SRD). The SRD is more demanding than the trading book rules, since it always requires banks to have at least 8% own funds. The CAD initially followed the building block approach for measuring market risk: risk in interest rate and equity instruments is added to counterpart and settlement risk for the total risk exposure calculation. This directive was, however, seen as much too detailed and was later overtaken by new developments in supervision of trading activities of banks and investment firms, the internal models or Value-at-Risk (VAR) approach. This new approach was accepted by the Basle Committee on Banking Supervision in the 1995 Amendment to the Basle Capital Accord to Incorporate Market Risk and became operational from 1998 onwards. It allows banks, under certain conditions, to control their market exposure through their own models. The CAD was consequently amended to take the VAR models into account (CAD II). However, even the VAR will need to be further refined, as became evident during the September 1998 emerging market crisis. Many models had not taken account of the likelihood of such an exceptional situation. This raises the further problem of a flexible framework for financial regulation. The EU legislative procedure typically takes at least two years to have a proposal adopted, with another year for national implementation.

In insurance, potential claims of policy-holders are backed by technical provisions that are set to cover the anticipated claims and associated costs arising from the policies underwritten. The third-generation insurance directives introduced minimum rules for the qualitative and quantitative investment of assets. The directives specify the list of admissible assets and the required level of diversification. Investments must take account of the type of business carried on by an undertaking in such a way as to secure their safety, yield and marketability. They must be adequately diversified and spread ('prudent man' rule). Requirements to invest in particular categories of assets are abolished and replaced by minimum rules for the investment of technical reserves, the list of admissible assets to cover these reserves, their diversification and valuation. Maximum percentages apply for cash (<3%), unlisted securities (<10%), and the total of single large holdings or loans (large exposures). Member states can lay down more detailed rules on the acceptable assets for firms under their supervision, which is for example the case for investments in equity, but this should not hinder EU-licensed firms from countries with more liberal regimes in offering their services on its territory. The directives also contain rules on currency matching, which prohibit insurance firms from holding more than 20% of their assets denominated in currencies that do not match the currency denominations of the liabilities. Moreover, insurance companies are required to maintain a solvency margin, or a buffer that they need to maintain to cover unexpected losses and costs.

Pension funds are not included in the EU regulatory framework for financial services. A draft directive liberalising the management and investment of pension funds in the EU had to be withdrawn by the European Commission in 1994, as a result of broad disagreements between the member states.[10] The draft pension funds directive contained only qualitative rules for the spread of investments in the EU and a lower currency matching rule than the life insurance directives, which represented the main stumbling block of the proposal. This directive would have favoured retirement savings in the form of pension funds, as compared to group insurance schemes, which are subject to the rules of the life insurance directives. Some member states with pension funds, such as Denmark, have, however, made their pension funds subject to the rules of the life insurance directives, but most other member states with pension funds have kept them under a separate legal regime. Restrictions on pension fund investments have not yet been harmonised.

The free provision and cross-border recognition of securities instruments is covered by a series of directives covering unit trusts, listing prospectuses and initial public offerings (IPOs). Whereas the harmonised legal regime has worked for unit trusts, it is much less complete for primary securities instruments. The latter issue is analysed in detail in Chapter 4, as part of the policy issues to be considered for an integrated capital market to work. Free provision of unit trusts was instituted by the 1985 UCITS directive (undertakings for collective investment in transferable securities), which sets minimum standards to allow for a single licence for the sale of UCITS throughout the Community. Member states that apply more stringent standards may not forbid the sale on their territory of UCITS authorised in another member state. The directive sets out harmonised rules for the composition, management and investment of UCITS as well as the information requirements. National marketing and tax rules do not fall within the scope of this directive. They remain under host country control, which means that UCITS must still comply with national regulations in that respect. Two draft amendments under consideration in the EU Council extend the single licence to the companies managing UCITS and the types of funds that can be considered as UCITS. The first draft harmonises the prudential rules for companies managing funds and allows cross-border management of funds with a single licence, thus making a step towards an EU-wide pension fund market. The second allows new forms of UCITS such as funds investing in bank deposits and other highly liquid financial assets.

New Priorities

Overall, home country control has worked in integrating markets. The problems that have emerged thus far in the functioning of the single market have been of a different nature, and have mainly affected specific products: they relate to the impossibility or irrelevance of buying financial products in other markets because of regulatory or tax barriers. Or they have been caused by loopholes in the regulatory framework, such as the 'general good' issue. The European Commission has in the meantime acted on the latter issue, whereas the other remaining barriers are more difficult to tackle. At the retail level, they are one of the reasons for the continuing price differences for financial services in the EU and have resulted in calls for further regulation, most notably by consumer groups. At the level of securities products, problems with mutual recognition of prospectuses and IPOs will increasingly emerge as securitisation develops in the euro zone.

Financial institutions operating with a single licence since 1992 have often been hindered in particular member states by restrictions justified on the grounds of the 'general good' or by the notification procedure to host country authorities. Member states have prohibited the exercise of certain activities or the sale of certain products on their territory, alleging that these activities and products go against the general interest, or that the notification procedure was not duly respected. Both clauses, which form part of all key free-provision-of-services directives, have proved to be serious barriers to market integration, leading the Commission to adopt an interpretative Communication to define the circumstances in which they could be invoked in the banking sector.[11] The interpretation has been characterised as a 'courageous initiative' (Dassesse 1997), and is now being followed by an interpretative Communication for the insurance directives as well and, probably, for the investment services directive.

Another exception to home country control in the second banking directive (SBD) should disappear in EMU. According to Art. 14 of the SBD, host countries retained responsibility for the liquidity control of branches of credit institutions for monetary policy reasons. Now that monetary union has come into effect, there should be no reason to maintain this provision, although there has been no indication yet in this direction by local authorities.

Tax differences have proved more difficult to tackle, but will become even more distorting with monetary union. Deliberations within the Monti Group of the Commission have recently allowed some headway to be made in this area, but it will take some time before markets become truly integrated from the tax point of view. Products from host countries are of interest only if they are cheaper than those provided by local providers *after tax*. Tax relief for interest payments does not apply across borders. Agreement on a minimum level of withholding tax on interest income, proposed again by the European Commission in 1998, and to be implemented in 2001, will be a big step forward; but it will only be a first step.

Thus far, the single-market programme in financial services has not led to more convergence in the pricing of financial services in EU member states, as cross-border surveys for banking and insurance services prove.[12] Although the non-appearance of price convergence for financial services might have been caused by elements outside the SMP package for the financial sector, it has certainly contributed to consumer disenchantment with the single financial market and provoked calls for more regulation. This disenchantment was evident in the adoption of a directive for cross-border payment transfers (directive 97/5/EC), and other elements might be tackled in the near future. In a recent Communication, the European Commission (June 1997) proposed a series of measures to enhance consumer confidence in the single financial market. Highest on the list are the regulation of distance contracts for financial services, unregulated financial intermediaries, insurance agents, motor insurance abroad and electronic payments. Progress on consumer information and redress procedures will be followed-up in other areas as well.

Separately, the European Commission also indicated that pension funds should enjoy the freedoms of the single market. The investment and management of pension funds should be liberalised and remaining investment restrictions abolished. The European Commission relaunched the discussion with the publication of a Green Paper in June 1997 and will possibly adopt a new proposal for a directive in the near future.

NOTES

1. This principle does not apply to voting on financial matters (distribution of profits or loss) for which a special key, based on objective criteria (GDP and population weights), is used (Article 28) and whereby members of the Executive Board have no vote.
2. See ECB (1998).
3. Council Regulation (EC) No. 2531/98 concerning the application of minimum reserves by the ECB, *Official Journal*, 27.11.1998. The Council Regulation specifies three aspects of the ESCB's minimum reserve system, namely the reserve base, the maximum permissible reserve ratio and the sanctions to be imposed in cases of non-compliance. All other features of the system may be decided upon by the ECB within the limits set by the Statute of the ESCB and the Council Regulation. The ECB Regulation on the application of minimum reserves, adopted on 1 December 1998, defines the applicable reserve ratios, the institutions subject to reserve requirements, the calculation of reserve requirements, and the remuneration of holdings of required reserves.
4. See ECB web site (www.ecb.int) for more information and continuous updates of the eligible assets.
5. Examples of regulations are the 1989 merger control regulation, which gives the Commission direct powers to control the compatibility of European mergers with EU competition policy, or the draft European Company Statute, discussed below.
6. The list of credit institutions which fall under the scope of the directives is regularly updated and published in the official journal of the EC.

7. See annex of the investment services directive.

8. In banking and insurance, the free provision of services directives refer to a first generation directive which instituted the freedom of establishment across the EU.

9. An amendment to the solvency ratios directive was recently approved by the EU Council, generalising the 50% weighting for all forms of mortgage loans, depending on the approval of the home country authorities.

10. See Lannoo (1996) for a detailed overview of the objectives of the draft directive and the reasons for its withdrawal.

11. Commission Interpretative Communication, Freedom to provide services and the interest of the general good in the second banking directive, *OJ* C 209 of 10.7.1997.

12. See, for example: European Commission (1977c), *The Single Market Review: Credit Institutions and Banking*, Vol. 2, Kogan Page: London.

2
European Capital Markets at the Start of EMU

As can be witnessed in emerging markets, capital markets do not emerge from scratch. In the early phase, strong intermediaries are needed to channel savings to productive investments. Hence the crucial role of the banking sector. In Europe, the banking sector has remained dominant so far, which has hampered the development of capital markets. The first section of this chapter gives an overview of the different components of capital markets and their importance in Europe: equity, bond, derivatives and money markets; the second section discusses the role of the different intermediaries, banks, institutional investors and clearing and settlement agents.

EUROPEAN CAPITAL MARKETS: AN OVERVIEW

Stock Markets

Although the combined GDP of the EU is higher than that of the US, its total stock market capitalisation amounted to only 55% of US stock market capitalisation at the end of 1998. When one excludes the UK, the figure drops to 37%. Europe's share of world market capitalisation amounts to about 25%, compared to 49% for North America and 17% for East and South-East Asia. Therefore, European stock markets should have a lot of growth potential in terms of the proportion of the economy that is traded on organised exchanges.

Europe currently hosts 31 national stock exchanges (not including the regional or specialised exchanges), of which 15 are in the EU, compared to 8 in the US (where two major exchanges, NYSE and NASDAQ, command 95% of the business).[1] Their relative importance differs highly and generalisations are difficult to make. Fundamental differences exist in their local role, international orientation, trading techniques and governance. They reflect differences in the origin of the exchanges, in corporate finance and shareholding structures, in the role of financial intermediaries and the competitive strength of financial centres.

At the end of 1998, market capitalisation of domestic stock, expressed as a percentage of GDP, ranged from 156% in the UK and 152% in the Netherlands to 49% in Germany and 46% in Italy (see Graph 2.1 and Table A1.1 in the Statistical Appendix).[2] The number of domestic listed companies ranged from 2,399 in the UK to 741 in Germany, 700 in France and 239 in Italy. Overall, the average stock market capitalisation in the EU falls well below the levels registered in the US. By the end of 1998, the 15 member states of the EU had a domestic stock market capitalisation of 80% of GDP, compared to 145% in the US (NYSE and NASDAQ). Excluding the UK, the average stock market capitalisation in the EU amounts to 64% of GDP. The number of domestic listed companies in the EU comes closer to the figure for the US, NYSE and NASDAQ taken jointly. The total number of listed companies stood at 6,251 by the end of 1998, as compared to 2,278 for NYSE and 4,572 for NASDAQ. The difference *within* the EU, however, between the UK on the one hand and the other member states on the other, is considerable.

Some countries are notable exceptions to the low levels of stock market capitalisation observed in continental Europe. In the Netherlands, Sweden and Switzerland, for example, the levels stand much higher than in other continental European countries and reach Anglo-Saxon standards. Moreover, a

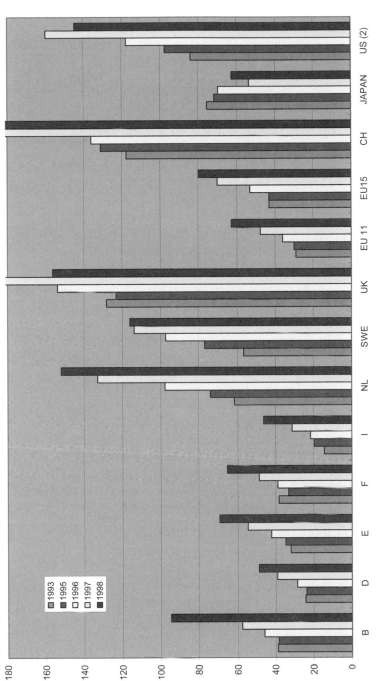

Graph 2.1 *Stock market capitalisation as % of GDP (domestic listed companies, end of year)*
Sources: FESE, FIBV, European Commission. The data for the US refer to NYSE and NASDAQ

marked increase in market capitalisation as a percentage of GDP can be observed in these countries in recent years, rising between 1993 and 1998 from 62% to 152% in the Netherlands, from 57% to 116% in Sweden and from 118% to 238% in Switzerland. The higher ratios for these smaller countries reflect differences in corporate culture, company law and average size of corporations.

Other European countries have in the meantime started to catch up, indicating that a more market-based system might be emerging. Levels of stock market capitalisation have been rising in the big continental European countries since 1997. Also the number of listed companies has risen significantly, although not equally across the EU. In the EU15, the total number of locally listed companies on the main national stock exchanges increased from 5,343 in 1995 to 6,251 in 1998. Such figures have, however, to be considered with care. Companies can disappear from the stock exchange as a result of a merger, new ones appear in IPOs or demergers. Over a longer time period, the strongest net increases can be noticed in Germany, Italy, Sweden and Switzerland (see Table A1.3 in Appendix 1).

Stock exchanges also differ significantly in their interest and ability in attracting foreign listings. Foreign listings do not exist in some exchanges while they are of major importance in others. The number of foreign listed companies in Germany is higher than the domestic, but with a low value of trading. In the UK, the value of trading in foreign equity is higher than in domestic equity. London accounts for 93% of all foreign trading (1998) in the EU, which reflects the competitive strength of the City.

Equity turnover statistics have to be taken with care, however. Methods for calculating turnover differ, and there is much double-counting. Two systems are used: the 'regulatory environment view' (REV), which incorporates all trades over which an exchange has regulatory oversight, and the 'trading system view' (TSV), which only counts trades passing through a specific trading system. According to Steil (1996), double-counting in London's foreign equity turnover is caused by double reporting of trades to the stock exchange, even if the trade did not take place there. German figures are inflated by

the specific local structure of trading through different inter-
acting intermediaries, in which the same trade might be
reported more than once. Turnover statistics also do not include
trading that occurs off-exchange, which used to be most
common in Italy and Germany (FESE 1990).

In the past, trading systems differed on a geographical basis,
but they have now largely converged. London used the dealer
market or quote-driven system, whereas all other continental
European exchanges had a continuous auction or an order-
driven system. In the London stock market, market-makers set
buy and sell prices for stocks. This was seen as an attractive
system for institutional investors, since they can execute large
trades at a pre-announced price. In 1986, the London Stock
Exchange created SEAQ International, a screen-based quotation
system specialising in non-British stocks. It offered continuous
trading, a very liquid market and a familiar environment for
institutional investors. One year later, the stock exchange went
through the 'Big Bang', which liberalised market access and
pricing. As a result, the competitiveness of the London
Exchange increased considerably and it won much trade in
European stocks from the continental European exchanges. For
most of 1990, for example, SEAQ managed to control more than
half of all the trading in Dutch and Swedish stocks (Pagano
1998).

In reaction to the competition from London, continental
exchanges invested heavily in the improvement of their auction
system. The latter system works on the basis of continuous
matching of buy and sell orders. It is cheaper for small orders
than the quote-driven system, but large orders could lead to
significant temporary price changes in the former open outcry
floor trading system. The threat of losing more business to
London led to the introduction of computerised continuous
screen-based trading and the liberalisation of market access and
commissions. Some exchanges also introduced elements of the
dealer market system to attract large trades.

Overall, continental European exchanges succeeded in
winning back trade from London. Bid-ask spreads by London
brokers increased, as a result of the growing strength and
efficiency of the continental European auction systems: broker-

dealers were less willing and able to act as direct counterparts for their clients' orders and to commit capital, as compared to merely executing orders in the auction systems. In October 1997, London introduced an automated order-driven system (SETS), to run in parallel with the dealership market for large trades. Over a decade, trading systems on European exchanges converged towards a common dualistic structure, with automated auction systems for small and medium-sized stocks and a market-making segment for large trades (Pagano 1998).

The implementation of the EC's investment services directive (ISD) signalled a further reorientation of trades to the domestic exchange, but not necessarily to local intermediaries. The ISD allows investment firms to provide their services all over the EU with a single licence, and stock exchanges to place their automated facilities in the other EU member states (the 'remote access'). Brokers or dealers can act on a host country's stock exchange without being established there. Stock exchanges can place screens with intermediaries in other member states. This removes a significant deterrent to cross-border trading and allows business to be transacted where it can be done most cheaply, in principle on a firm's domestic exchange, where liquidity is the highest. The proliferation in the use of the Internet will extend these facilities to the retail market.

Bond Markets

From its launch, the euro became the second most important currency in international bond markets, with a share of about one-third of all publicly issued bonds if one just adds the national markets. This is still well below the US dollar which garnered 44.5% of total bonds outstanding in the major bond markets in 1996 (see Table 2.1).[3] However, the critical mass effect could also play in the bond markets: a broader used currency and more liquid capital market could attract more issues than the sum of the component currencies before, as seems to be the case so far in the first months of EMU.

The US dollar sector was more than 2.6 times greater than

Table 2.1   *World bond markets by currency, 1996 ($ billions)*

USD (bn)	Total	% of global	Public	% of global	Private	% of global	Ratio public/ private
USD	9,583.4	44.5	6,366.4	47.8	3,217	39.2	1.98
JAY	3,655.9	17.0	2,245.5	16.8	1,410.4	17.2	1.59
DEM	2,303.1	10.7	838.6	6.3	1,464.5	17.8	0.57
ITL	1,274.4	5.9	998.8	7.5	275.6	3.4	3.62
FRF	1,044	4.8	731.8	5.5	312.2	3.8	2.34
Other EMU	1,429.7	6.6	836.6	6.3	593.1	7.2	1.41
UKP	661.8	3.1	446.6	3.4	215.2	2.6	2.08
Other EU non-EMU	599	2.8	278.3	2.1	320.7	3.9	0.87
CAD	446.3	2.1	313.1	2.3	133.2	1.6	2.35
Other	549.9	2.6	275.3	2.1	274.6	3.3	1.00
Global	21,547.5	100	13,331	100	8,216.5	100	1.62
EU 15	7,312	33.9	4,130.7	31	3,181.3	38.7	1.30
EU 11	6,051.2	28.1	3,405.8	26	2,645.4	32.2	1.29

Source: Salomon Brothers (1997); data do not include Treasury bills.

the second largest market in 1996, the Japanese yen bond market. The total EU 15 currencies' share amounted to 33.9% (including the ECU bonds), with 5.9% for 'pre-in' countries (Denmark, Greece, Sweden and the UK). The share of the dollar sector has slowly declined since the 1970s, with some interruptions. A further fall due to an increased share of the euro would thus only prolong an already existing historical trend.

Public bonds represent the largest share of total debt outstanding in world bond markets, accounting for 62% in 1996, compared to 38% for private sector debt. The US dollar share is slightly higher in this sector, with 47.8% of all public bonds. EU currencies' share is lower, at 31%. The EU currencies' share is higher in central government debt at 42.5%, with 9% for the 'opt-outs'.

In private bonds, EU currencies garnered 38.7% of all debt outstanding, compared to 39.2% for the dollar. Above all, DEM has an important share in this sector, which is caused by the German *Pfandbriefe*, the securitised mortgage loans and communal debt, which had a total volume outstanding of $923bn by the end of 1996. *Pfandbriefe* have only been issued as international bonds since early 1996. It is interesting to note that the total of public sector bonds issued by the EU 11 govern-ments is usually much smaller than for the US although the GDP of the euro area is similar to that of the US, and euro area countries have a much higher debt/GDP ratio. The main reason for this apparent contradiction is that not all 'Maastricht' debt is incorporated in securities, and not all securities issued by euro area governments are tradable.

As far as total volumes of public debt are concerned, Italy's share amounts to 26% of the total tradable debt outstanding of the EU member states (BIS, June 1998). Germany comes second, with 17%, followed by France (15%) and the UK (10%). The total volume of the non-EMU states amounts to 19%. Most of this debt is placed in domestic debt securities. The five largest EU member states, which account for threequarters of the total volume of outstanding debt, have less than 5% placed in inter-national debt securities. The share is higher for the smaller member states, especially Sweden and Finland, which have more than one-third of their debt in international bonds. These states needed to go to the international market, since the take-up in the local market was too limited. Domestic ownership of government debt stands at 37% in Finland and 54% in Sweden, as compared to 70 to 80% in the other EU markets (see Table A1.4 in Appendix 1).

The average maturity of government debt stands at about 5 years for the EU, with lows for Sweden with 2.6 years and highs for the UK with 10.1 years. Low levels of maturity can aggra-vate short-term liquidity problems in public finance, and this often leads rating firms to lower sovereign ratings. The foreign currency component of public debt is limited to 6.5% in the EU. In some smaller member states, it is much higher, and reached 32% in Sweden and 50% in Finland in 1997, before EMU thus!

The Former Euro-bond Market

Euro-bonds, in the former sense of the word, are international bonds issued by a syndicate of securities houses in any inter-national currency and placed in more than one country.[4] The origins of the Euro-bond market can be traced back to the early 1960s, when a Euro-dollar bond market emerged as a result of tight US capital market regulations, the accumulation of offshore dollar balances and sizeable outward investment by US multinationals. By the end of the 1960s, a thriving DEM sector of the Euro-bond market had also been created, which was stimulated by the existence of withholding taxes on domestic German bonds. Towards the mid-1970s, the Euro-bond market had consolidated its position: a trading infrastructure had been established for the Euro-bond market, and London had become the centre of a large and active market for Euro-dollars. By the end of 1997, the total amount of Euro-bonds outstanding amounted to $2,697bn (11.2% of total publicly issued bonds outstanding). The largest currency in 1996 continued to be the dollar (39%), with the most important non-dollar sections in DEM (15%) and yen (12%).

An important characteristic and source of competitive advantage of the Euro-bond market is the non-application of withholding taxes. This issue is discussed in more detail below (see Box 4.1 in Chapter 4). Another advantage of the Euro-bond market—at least for the issuer—is that it is subject to less regulation. But what securities can benefit from this lighter regime? It has not always been very clear for tax authorities and statisticians to decide when bonds can be classified as being 'Euro', international or domestic. In some cases, issuers had to go through foreign subsidiaries for issues to be recognised as Euro-bonds by the tax authorities. The UK tax authorities have lifted this requirement in recent years and do not apply withholding taxes for Euro-bonds held by the international clearing bodies CEDEL or Euroclear. In the case of Luxembourg, its emergence as the Euro-bond listing centre was based on the absence of withholding taxes on interest income.

In EU legislation, the definition of Euro-bonds was harmonised in the 1989 prospectus directive. This directive sets out the information that must be published for all forms of securities sold to the public. It defines Euro-securities as transferable securities that are underwritten by a syndicate from at least two members from different states, are offered on a significant scale in one or more member states other than the issuer's registered office, and may be acquired initially only by a financial institution. Other commonly accepted criteria are those employed by the International Financing Review (IFR). It determines that an issue shall be a public offering with customary Euro-documentation; full disclosure of the terms of the issue; a listing on a recognised international stock exchange; and eligibility for clearing through a recognised clearing system. Sole manager issues do not qualify as Euro-bonds, according to the IFR criteria. Differences in accounting standards have, however, made the mutual acceptance of prospectus details difficult, as discussed below.

Money and Foreign Exchange Markets

The first weeks of the eurosystem saw a quick move towards an integrated interbank market, with generalised use of euribor, the interbank money market interest rate benchmark, taking effect. Spreads across the different national interbank markets in the euro zone declined rapidly to about 10 basis points, indicating that banks have started to manage their liquidity more centrally and operate in the euro area as a single financial market. Another indication in this direction was the wide use of collateral on a cross-border basis for operations with central banks in the eurosystem. TARGET, the wholesale payment system of the ESCB, had a stronger take-off than expected, with some 25,000 cross-border payments a day (and an average value of payments of 900bn euro a day) and a market share of 70% in large value payments, with about one-third cross-border.

Euribor, the benchmark for money market interest rates in the euro zone, was developed by a group of banks within the European banking federation.[5] In addition the British Bankers Association developed its euro-Libor, but even for London-based institutions, such as the futures exchanges Liffe, Euribor rapidly became the benchmark. For the euro overnight index swap market, Eonia (Euro Overnight Index Average) applies. Eonia is calculated with the help of the ESCB as a weighted average of all overnight unsecured lending transactions in the euro area interbank market. The London equivalent is Euronia.

The big difference with the situation ex-ante is the depth and liquidity of the euro cash market and the associated derivatives. Foreign exchange risks and commissions were immediately eliminated within the euro area, which should create huge savings for business.[6] Furthermore, accounts can be rationalised and centralised in banking (nostro accounts) as well as in corporate treasury services. The existence of several euro cross-border payment systems will facilitate this process. The ESCB offers the TARGET system with immediate finality, others are net settlement systems with end-of-day clearance, such as the EBA (Euro Banking Association) system.

EMU should lead to the further development of private repo markets in Europe. In the US, private repo markets form an important alternative to money market instruments. Repos facilitate short-term financing by providing access to secured borrowings. This allows finance houses to improve their leveraging by lending out securities for cash. In Europe, the most important repo'd assets are government bonds, with more than half of the market share, followed by Euro-bonds (ISMA 1997). The most liquid repo markets were in France, where the authorities have encouraged their development, and in the UK, where they were imported by American banks. The German repo business was until recently located in London, because of the existence of reserve requirements in Germany. But this has changed in the meantime.

Monetary union should give the private repo market the liquidity and depth it has lacked so far. The generalised use of repurchase agreements by the ECB and the harmonisation of eligible paper for liquidity-providing operations will provide the necessary framework for a private euro-repo market to emerge. Its development, however, depends on some other elements as well, such as market conventions (the existence of stripped bonds), clearing facilities and withholding tax regulations.

In the foreign exchange markets, the dominance of the dollar is not likely to diminish rapidly, owing to its role as a vehicle currency. Until the early 1980s, the dollar was the sole vehicle currency. All transactions in the interbank market between currencies without a liquid bilateral market went through the dollar as the vehicle currency. This inflates the USD volume to a much higher level than justified through fundamentals. Peter Kenen (quoted in Hartmann 1996) estimated that between 90 and 99% of all interbank foreign exchange turnover in 1980 had the dollar on one side of the transaction (on a total of 200%, since each transaction involves two currencies). The picture changed through the emergence of the DEM as a second vehicle currency. The DEM's role as a vehicle was, however, largely limited to trading between European currencies, whereas the dollar has liquid interbank markets with practically all other currencies, serving as a global vehicle currency (Hartmann 1996). The Japanese yen on the other hand does not play any role as a foreign exchange vehicle currency, not even between Asian currencies, where the dollar is still dominant.

At the end of 1995, the dollar had a share of 83.8% of all foreign exchange transactions (on a total of 200%), the DEM 37.1% and the yen 23.6%. Other EU currencies' share amounted to 32.8%. In *spot* foreign exchange, the share of the DEM amounted to 54.3%, the dollar to 71.1%, while the yen was at about the same level. This difference is due to the more limited role of the DEM in forward markets (Hartmann 1996).

Will the euro supplant the dollar as the main vehicle currency? This is unlikely, because the euro inherited few vehicle trades from the DEM, since intra-European trading disappeared under EMU. The euro's vehicle role will mostly come into play with EU currencies which are not part of EMU from the beginning or with other European non-EU currencies, such as the CHF and NOK, and the currencies from Central and Eastern European countries (CEECs).

The decrease in the intra-EMU foreign exchange business occurred well before EMU started. Rate spreads between the prospective EMU members had already become minimal from early 1998 onwards and business had shifted to other currencies. The disappearance of the intra-EMU forex business hit financial centres unequally: it was estimated that those centres that derived most of their income from trade among European currencies would be most affected. Paris, Madrid, Milan, Amsterdam and Stockholm, for example, probably lost more than 50% of their forex business. London, the world's most important forex centre (32% of global foreign exchange turnover), would have been less affected, although it may still have lost importantly in volume terms.[7]

Before the introduction of the euro, the role of European currencies as an official reserve currency was limited. In official holdings of foreign exchange, the DEM had a 13.7% share, compared to 56.4% for the dollar (1995). Other European currencies, such as the FRF and GBP, had shares of 1.8% and 3.4% respectively (Masson and Turtelboom 1997). The share of the dollar was at around 80% in the 1970s, but subsequently declined and has remained at today's level for the last decade. The share of dollar reserves is somewhat higher in developing than in industrialised countries.

It has often been argued that the pooling of foreign exchange reserves in the ECB would lead to downward pressures on the dollar. Since the reserve needs of the ECB are much lower than the reserves available with participating central banks, large amounts of excess dollar reserves would be dumped into the market, resulting in a considerable fall of the dollar. The overall amounts of excess official reserves should not be exaggerated, however, compared to the sums going daily through international money markets. Furthermore, as already evidenced in early 1999, other factors are much more important in determining the external value of the euro, such as the economic climate, the monetary policy stance and the credibility of the ECB. Shifts in central banks' foreign exchange reserves should not cause market upheavals (Masson and Turtelboom 1997).

Derivative Markets

Futures exchanges are obvious victims of EMU. In 1998, there were 23 futures and options exchanges in Europe (compared to 7 in the US), offering derivative instruments based on currencies, short- and long-term interest rates, and equities. The most important European derivative exchanges are, in order of importance, Eurex (merger of Frankfurt's DTB and the Swiss

Soffex), London (Liffe), and the options exchange of the Amsterdam stock exchange (AEX). A decade ago, futures and options exchanges were insignificant in Europe, but they have caught up with their American counterparts in the meantime. European futures exchanges have become important players, with the Eurex and Liffe ranking second and fifth, respectively, world-wide in 1998 on the basis of the total volume of contracts traded, preceded only by the Chicago derivative markets (CBOT, CME and CBOE) (Table 2.2).

Derivative markets emerged only 25 years ago, and can be considered as one of the most revolutionary innovations in finance of the last decades, comparable to equity exchanges in previous centuries. Their emergence is linked to the break-down on the Bretton Woods Exchange Rate Agreement and the increase in exchange and interest rate volatility. The Chicago Board of Trade started in October 1975 with a contract on

Table 2.2   Top world derivative exchanges (1998)

		Exchange	1998 volume of contracts	1997 rank	Annual change
1	CBOT	(Chicago Board of Trade)	281,189,436	1	15.9
2	EUREX	(DTB/Soffex merger)	248,212,405	5	60.8
3	CME	(Chicago Mercantile Exchange)	226,618,806	3	12.9
4	CBOE	(Chicago Board Options Exchange)	206,865,991	4	10.5
5	LIFFE	(London International Financial Futures Exchange)	194,394,153	2	−7.2
6	AMEX	(American Stock Exchange)	97,644,992	7	10.8
7	BM&F	(Bolsa Brasileira de Futuros)	87,015,050	6	−28.8
8	NYMEX	(New York Mercantile Exchange)	76,482,995	8	19.6
9	AEX	(European Options Exchange, A'dam)	65,002,584	11	33.6
10	MONEP	(Marché des Options Négociables de Paris)	62,731,486	27	392.8

Source: *Futures and Options Weekly*, 1999.

mortgage-backed securities, followed 3 months later with a 3-month T-bill (short-term US Treasury certificate) contract. The development of options, although existing before, benefited strongly from the Black–Scholes formula (1973) on the pricing of options. Derivative markets made it possible to commoditise risk and hence to buy, sell, restructure and price risk in line with investors' preferences, separate from the underlying assets (Steinherr 1998: p. 28).

The top contracts in Europe are Eurex (DTB) Bund and Liffe's Euromark contract, which were ranked third and fourth, respectively, among the most traded contracts world-wide in 1998, after Chicago's US T-bond and Eurodollar contracts. In currency futures, the US futures exchanges (Chicago) dominate, in bonds futures the roles are split between the US exchanges and the leading European futures exchanges.

The competition between Liffe and Eurex has recently become very tough, with Eurex surpassing Liffe's 10-year dominance in the Bund contracts. The contracts traded hardly differ, but what differentiates the two is the trading technology: open outcry floor trading on Liffe (the classic form of trading intermediated by traders crying on the exchange floor), electronic trading on Eurex. It shows that the right trading environment, which increasingly features electronic trading, matters more than anything else in the localisation of derivatives markets. The fact that Eurex is based in Frankfurt (and Zurich) is irrelevant for most traders, who can be based anywhere in the world. By the end of 1998, Eurex had 313 members (up from 171 in August 1997), of which 149 were remote, meaning not based in Germany or Switzerland. As with the stock exchanges, the competition is mainly based upon improvements in technology. As a result of the competition from Eurex, Liffe announced that it would move to a hybrid structure, combining screen trading with open outcry.

Derivative exchanges are highly affected by EMU, because of the disappearance of exchange rate differentials and the convergence of interest rates. A number of foreign exchange and interest rate contracts have disappeared. An integrated bond market is likely to have a single yield curve. It should thus be served by a single futures contract, or a single contract at each maturity. Parallel euro future contracts in, for example, French and German government bonds will be superfluous.

INTERMEDIARIES IN EUROPEAN CAPITAL MARKETS

The two most important intermediaries in capital markets are banks and institutional investors. Institutional investors are commonly defined as financial institutions that invest their clients' money on a longer-term basis, such as insurance companies, pension funds and investment funds. They are distinct from banks, which take short-term deposits from clients. The distinction is to a certain extent artificial, however, since it does not take into account the differences in the structure of the financial services industry in the EU or the changes that have taken place since the late 1980s. In some countries, banks increasingly provide a whole series of financial services, ranging from traditional banking products, to insurance policies and investment vehicles. The insurance sector is experiencing a similar evolution, but in the other direction. Since banking and insurance remain separately authorised legal structures, their relative importance can easily be compared on the basis of aggregate information per country. It should also be noted that banks in some countries possess important equity stakes in industry and therefore fulfil the same role as investment banks in other countries.

The forces that have transformed financial institutions in the last decades in Europe and elsewhere throughout the world can be summarised in two words: globalisation and technology. Globalisation is the effect of the world-wide liberalisation of markets, by which the world becomes the market. In the area of finance, it requires the free movement of capital and freedom of establishment. These principles were recently institutionalised in the GATS agreement for the financial services sector, and concluded in the World Trade Organisation in Geneva on 12 December 1997. The EU's single market programme is an element of globalisation, since it liberalises trade in financial services in the EU—to a much greater extent than at the world-wide level. Globalisation has increased competition and reduced margins for financial institutions, requiring them to adjust their size.

Technological developments are an important contributor to this process. From being a tool, technology has become an enabler to add value and reduce risk. As a result of technological progress, banks and institutional investors can act on world capital markets, while at the same time controlling and integrating their global risk exposure. Back-office operations have become predominantly paperless and fully automated. At the retail level, automation has advanced at an enormous pace, making the traditional types of distribution networks, namely branches, less important. In less than a decade, automatic cash dispensers and direct debit cards have become an element of everyday life. The Internet is a further step in the direction of virtual banks, allowing customers to execute all forms of financial operations from a personal computer at home.

Technology requires huge investments, which have contributed to the consolidation process in the financial sector. Large US banks annually spend over $1bn on technology. According to a recent study, technological progress has had a positive impact on reducing European banking costs by about 3% per annum between 1988 and 1995, but large banks benefited more than their smaller counterparts did (Molyneux 1997). Technological progress has affected efficient bank size, since the overall cost saving increases with the size of the bank. This cost reduction effect of new technologies should continue further in the decade ahead, with the rapid growth of low-cost hardware and software.

In restructuring their activities, financial institutions have started to focus on productive efficiency, on better internal capital allocation and risk management, and, finally, on higher profitability and shareholder value. To attract the huge sums needed to finance their expansion plans, financial institutions have to prove they can produce value for their investors, hence the increased attention to return on equity (ROE) also seen in European banking. In strategic marketing, financial institutions have reassessed their strategies in such key areas as improving customer focus and enhancing service quality.

Financial institutions have pursued different strategies as a result of this drive towards higher efficiency and customer focus. Some have pursued a strategy of *Allfinanz*, whereas others have concentrated on their core business and the development of niche markets. The former strategy is the one most in evidence, although it is probably the most publicised as well. By following the *Allfinanz* concept, financial institutions want to generate economies of scope by providing banking, insurance and asset management services. This approach is a particularly effective way for banks with extensive branch networks to increase their productivity. Bank-insurance needs to be qualified, since only standardised insurance products can usefully be sold via banks, such as life, fire and car insurance, often linked to a typical bank product, such as a mortgage or car loan. Modules of such standardised products can be stored on the networks of banks, again allowing a more extensive use of technology while reducing processing errors. More specific insurance policies are left for insurance companies or brokers.

The data on mergers and acquisitions in the financial sector provide evidence of this consolidation process. The total number of mergers and acquisitions increased sharply from the announcement of the single market programme onwards, and has subsequently been maintained at high levels, reaching unprecedented levels in 1998. This was a result not only of the advent of EMU, but also of a global tendency for concentration. In the US as well as in Europe, banking was the most merger-intensive sector in 1998; insurance the sixth most merger-intensive in the US, and the third in Europe. Concentration is still higher intersector than across sectors, although more than one third of all deals (36%) in the financial services sector in Europe in the period 1985–1997 was a cross sector, as compared to 15% in the US. For the US, this is due to the restrictions on cross-sectoral and interstate (for insurance) integration. Regulatory reform of the 1933 US Glass–Steagall Act has been under discussion in Congress for five years and is now concretely challenged by the Travellers–Citigroup merger. In Europe, bank consolidation has mainly remained national. In the insurance sector, on the other hand, the cross-border element has dominated, as several European and international mergers and acquisitions have occurred lately (Danthine, Giavazzi, Vives and von Thadden 1999: p. 55).

Academic studies have found no conclusive evidence concerning the economic effects of large banking mergers. Diseconomies of scale arise for large banks in several European member states. There is also evidence of diseconomies of scope for bank-insurance companies. The main positive effect of mergers might be the improvement of operational efficiency (X-efficiencies) through cost reductions (Molyneux, Gardener and Van der Vennet 1997). This was confirmed in a more recent study, which found a higher degree of cost efficiency in universal banks and conglomerates as compared to more specialised banks. Despecialisation may thus lead to more efficient financial systems (Van der Vennet 1998).

As a result of this trend towards national consolidation, the levels of concentration in banking have increased to worrying levels in some markets. The best example is in the Netherlands, where five groups control 80% of the banking market (see Table 2.3). In the insurance sector, on the other hand, concentration, measured as the market share of the five largest institutions,

Table 2.3 *Concentration in banking**

	1985	1990	1995	1997
B	48	48	54	57
DK	61	76	74	73
D		13.9	16.7	16.1
E	38.1	34.9	45.5	43.6
F	46	42.5	41.3	40.3
I	20.9	19.1	26.1	24.6
NL	69.3	73.4	76.1	79.4
A	35.9	34.6	39.2	48.3
P	61	58	74	76
SF	51.7	53.5	68.6	77.8
SW	60.2	70	85.9	89.7
UK			27	28
EU 11				10.8
EU 15				9.2
US		9	13	

* Defined as the asset share of the top five banks as a percentage of the total banking assets in a certain country. Data for EU 11 and EU 15 are 1996.

Source: De Bandt (1998), ECB (1999).

declined. Only in some markets did concentration in the insurance sector increase between 1992 and 1996, most markedly in Belgium (CEA 1998). The euro should reduce the danger of monopolistic or concerted practices in this respect, since it eliminates an important barrier to cross-border financial market integration. According to estimates for the EU 11, Euroland would start with a low degree of market concentration in the banking sector (10.8%, see Table 2.3), allowing scope for further consolidation. From a competition policy point of view, monitoring financial integration in Euroland to examine whether it works effectively as a single financial market is therefore crucial.

Banks

Unlike the situation in the US, banks dwarf institutional investors in Europe in asset terms, confirming Europe's position as a bank-based system. Important cross-country variations do, however, exist, with total bank assets equal to GDP in some countries, but two or even three times larger in others. In the US, commercial bank assets represent 62% of GDP (1996), with pension funds and investment funds having comparable sizes (see Graph 3.1 below). The gross value-added of the banking sector, calculated as gross income (net interest and non-interest income) as a percentage of GDP, varies less across EU countries, and amounted to 5% in the EU in 1996, as compared to 4.1% for the US commercial banks. Apart from Luxembourg, where the banking sector dominates the economy with a gross income of 39% of GDP, most countries have come closer to the average over time (see Table A1.5 in Appendix 1).

European banking has gone through a decade of far-reaching regulatory reform. The single market programme streamlined financial regulation at the EU level to allow for free cross-border branching and provision of services with a single licence. On the banking side of the business, the regulatory framework is well defined and complete. The single banking market measures, the second banking directive and related directives, came into force in time, that is in 1993. They follow the universal banking model and allow banks to undertake, apart from the traditional commercial banking activities, securities-related activities. Banks are also allowed to have shares in industry, going up to 60% of their own funds.

On the securities side of the business, the regulatory framework is more recent and less complete. The basic directives came into force in 1996 and implementation is still under way: the investment services directive, which defines the conditions for a single licence for non-bank investment firms, was only implemented in Spain and Germany in early 1998(!). The related capital adequacy directive sets capital requirements for these firms, but is also applicable to the trading books of universal banks. The level of harmonisation in the investment services directive has not been taken as far as it has in banking legislation, however, and market integration relies more on mutual recognition, as discussed below.

So far, structural changes in the banking industry in response to market liberalisation have been limited. For example, there has been little change in indicators such as the number of branches, employment or profitability *at the European level*. Bank profitability and employment have stayed at the same level since 1989, the first year for which data for most EU countries are available. The number of branches increased by 6% between 1990 and 1996. Furthermore, the price convergence for financial services, as forecast by Cecchini in 1988, has not yet materialised.[8] Cecchini found differences in the price for the same service of up to 200% in the EU. A postal survey, carried out with 115 EU banks as part of the Commission study on the effectiveness of the single market in banking (European Commission 1997c), found no real convergence in the prices of the same banking services as covered by the Cecchini study. On the contrary, the price differentials had increased in some cases, as with commissions and fees. The most common strategic response by banks to increased competition was found to be the introduction of new products and services and diversification of the product range into areas such as insurance and investment products. The cost structure associated with this product diversification is very heterogeneous and has reduced the transparency for consumers of the cost of financial services.

It is often assumed that one of the prime indicators of structural reform in banking would be a reduction of the extensive branch networks. This is not so obvious if one looks at the trends in the number of inhabitants per branch, which has so far declined almost continuously (i.e. the number of branches has continued to increase). In 1996, there were on average 1986 inhabitants per branch. The EU average, however, hides important differences in country-specific trends: some countries realised modest reductions in branch networks, whereas in others, an aggressive expansion was pursued. In Italy, for example, banks pursued a competitive growth strategy in response to the single market programme (SMP) and increased the number of branches, growing by 46% in the period 1990–1996. The wide diversity in the density of branch networks in the EU, which shows no sign of convergence yet, is more a sign of differences in the market situations in general and in savings habits in particular. For example, countries with high savings levels, such as Belgium, generally have more extensive branch networks.

The significance of the differences in the density of branch networks should thus not be overstated. Total personnel is a much more important cost factor. It can be noted that differences in bank employment as a percentage of total employment are much smaller (with the exception of Luxembourg, see Table A1.5). Seen in relation to productivity, probably only Spain looks overbanked. Whether a given number of employees are distributed over many small branches or a few larger ones is irrelevant.

A more useful indicator of potential trouble is a national comparison of bank profitability. There is evidence that some countries have already successfully restructured their banking sector in response to increased competition and market integration, while other countries have yet to even begin this process (Graph 2.2). Overall, according to the OECD statistics on bank profitability (1998), return on equity (ROE) of European banks remained at around 10% between 1990 and 1996. This status quo hides important national differences, however. Profitability decreased drastically in some southern European countries in the same period, reaching lows of 3.6% in France and 3.7% in Italy in 1995, and it was also low in Portugal and Switzerland. In the meantime, the competitive situation of banks in some northern European countries improved strongly, most markedly in the Netherlands, rising from 12.3% in 1990 to 17.6% in 1996, and the UK from 14.4% to 25.6% in the same period. Seen from a bank efficiency point of view, return on assets (ROA) is probably a better indicator, indicating the total return on the loan portfolio. On an average for 1994–1996, France ranks lowest again with 0.2%, followed by Belgium with 0.35% and Italy with 0.36% (excluding Finland, see Table A1.6 in Appendix 1). On both indicators, Europe is far below the US. US commercial banks realised a return on assets of 1.74% as compared to 0.49% for EU banks for the period 1994–1996. Return on equity stood at 21.6% for US banks compared to 9.8% for the EU over the same period.

Institutional Investors

The varying importance of institutional investors must be seen in the context of the regulatory framework for the provision of financial services and the way in which retirement plans are financed. The first explains the importance of investment funds in Luxembourg, since that country was the first to create a flexible regime for investment funds and does not tax interest income. The differences in the role of pension funds in the EU are explained by the second. Most European countries still have no pension funds of any significance, since pensions are largely financed on a pay-as-you-go basis, and the high level of replacement ratios in the official pension discourages the formation of additional privately sponsored funded plans (second pillar pensions).

Strong growth of the pension fund business has quite often been forecast for continental Europe. The overall demographic situation and the limits on public spending would favour the emergence of pension funds. Governments have, however, been rather slow in putting the necessary regulatory framework into place, or else the incentives for funded schemes to take off were

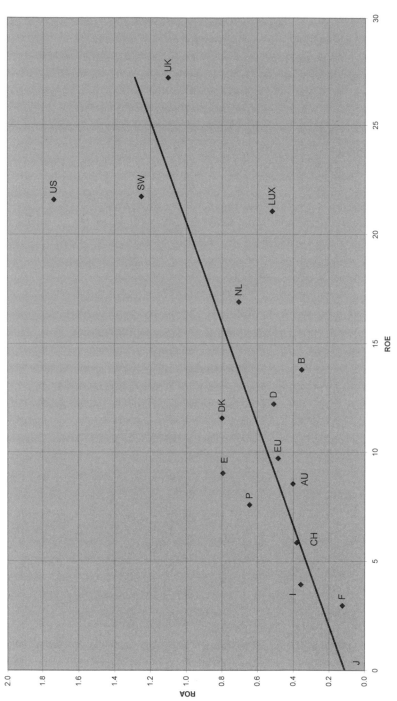

Graph 2.2 *Profitability in banking (average 1994–1996)*
Source: OECD (1998)

insufficient, which has impacted the growth of pension funds (see Table A1.8 in Appendix 1). The absence of a well-developed second pillar pension could also explain the importance of other forms of organised savings, such as investment funds in some countries, which could to a large extent be interpreted as individual retirement savings (third pillar pensions, see Table A1.9 in Appendix 1).

Nevertheless, EMU should spur growth of the asset management industry in Europe as a result of a greater drive towards securitisation and disintermediation. The emergence and development of a broader supply of debt and equity instruments in EMU will stimulate a broader pool of financial intermediaries. Such instruments have so far been unable to attain the critical mass needed for trading and liquidity in Europe. Increased competition for the savings pool will stimulate specialisation within the asset management industry.

In volume terms, insurance companies are the most important group of institutional investors, possessing total assets in the EU as high as pension funds and investment funds combined (see Table A1.7 in Appendix 1). In the US, the three groups are of a more comparable importance, with insurance companies being the least important. In relative terms, there are remarkable cross-country differences, with the southern EU countries and Finland having a much smaller insurance sector than the northern European countries. Pension funds are only of real importance in three EU countries, the Netherlands, the UK and Ireland, which have well-developed second pillar pension schemes. Over time, the strongest growth has been observed in the investment funds sector, with the total value of assets rising from Euro 316bn in 1987 to 1,741bn in 1997. Pension funds grew from Euro 781bn in 1992 to 1,412bn in 1996. Size-wise, EU investment funds are half, pension funds one-third, of their US counterparts.

Insurance Companies and Pension Funds

A key factor for insurance companies and pension funds in EMU is whether asset allocation will become more comparable and less biased towards the home market. EMU is a further step in the market integration process, since the 80% currency matching rules which the insurance directives contain have become irrelevant, allowing euro zone insurers to spread their assets in a larger currency area and allowing further specialisation on the asset management side. Non-euro-zone insurance firms, however, certainly in smaller markets such as Sweden and Denmark, find themselves in a rather precarious situation.

As indicated above, pension funds are not yet included in the EU regulatory framework for financial services, and will benefit less from increased diversification opportunities brought about by EMU. An overview of the most important quantitative restrictions on pension fund investments in Western Europe is given in Table 2.4.

So far, asset allocation of pension funds and life insurance companies has shown more similarities across countries than across sectors, as can be seen from Tables 2.5 and 2.6, with pension funds and insurance companies in the English-speaking countries investing over 50% of their assets in equity and those in continental European countries investing the biggest part in fixed income. Data on the distribution of assets of life insurance companies indicate an average investment of 67% in domestic

Table 2.4   *Most important quantitative restrictions on pension fund investments in Europe*

Belgium	>15% in government bonds
Denmark	Rules of the EU's third life insurance directive, 80% currency matching
France	>50% EU government bonds
Germany	<30% EU equities, <25% EU property, <6% non-EU equities, <6% non-EU bonds, <20% overall foreign assets, >80% currency matching
Italy	<20% liquid assets, <50% non-listed OECD securities, <5% non-OECD securities, >30% currency matching
Portugal	<40% in foreign equity
Switzerland	<50% real estate, <30% Swiss equities, <30% foreign loans, <25% foreign equities

Sources: De Ryck (1996); European Commission (1997b); and others.

Table 2.5 *Asset structure of life insurance companies (1994)*

	Equity (%)	Fixed income (%)	Real estate (%)	Liquidity (%)	Foreign assets (%)
DK	25	66	3	6	5
D	5	76	5	14	n.a.
E	2	55	10	33	n.a.
F	19	69	8	4	—
I	12	75	12	2	10
NL	14	75	6	6	6
SW	23	61	7	9	n.a.
UK	61	27	9	3	15

Note: Fixed income data for Germany and the Netherlands include loans.
Sources: European Commission (1997b) based on CEA and OECD data.

Table 2.6 *Asset structure of pension funds (1994)*

	Equity (%)	Fixed income (%)	Real estate (%)	Liquidity (%)	Foreign assets (%)
B	36	47	7	10	
DK	22	65	9	4	7
D	11	75	11	3	6
E	4	82	1	13	5
IRL	55	35	6	4	
NL	30	58	10	2	25
SW	32	47	8	13	12
UK	80	11	6	3	30
CH	11	64	16	9	
US	52	36	4	8	10
JAPAN	29	63	3	5	

Sources: De Ryck (1996), and European Commission (1997b).

fixed income and 9.5% in equity in Germany, Spain, France and Italy. This compares with 24% for domestic fixed income and 61% for equity in the UK. Moreover a strong home bias can be noted, with foreign assets forming a very limited part of the portfolios of institutional investors, with the exception of the UK and some smaller countries. This home bias is also the case in the US, albeit on a much larger market scale.

That asset allocation is determined more by country-specific patterns than by investment restrictions is suggested by the fact that German pension funds invest much less in equity than they are allowed to by law. This can also be observed in the case of the Netherlands, which has no quantitative restrictions on pension funds investments.

The differences in asset structure of pension funds may also be determined by differences in pension schemes. Ireland, the Netherlands, the UK and to a lesser extent the US, employ defined benefit schemes for pension plans, whereby the employee's pension is based on a certain percentage of his final salary. Other continental European countries rely more on defined contribution schemes, whereby accumulated contributions constitute the final pension, which is comparable to a life insurance annuity. Defined benefit schemes can result in an actuarial deficit, since the present value of the pension is independent of the fund's assets. Nevertheless, the future liabilities of such schemes are best matched by portfolios composing a significant proportion of equities, which give better returns over the long run.

Investment Funds

In relative terms, investment funds are most important in Luxembourg, because of its flexible unit trust regime and its tax haven status, followed by France and Spain (see Table A1.7 in Appendix 1). In these three countries, but also in the other southern EU countries, investment funds are more important in asset terms than insurance companies and pension funds. This can be explained by the absence of well-developed second pillar pension schemes, which stimulates private (individual) retirement saving (three pillar). Pensions in these countries are almost totally financed on a pay-as-you-go basis, and although a high level of state pension is foreseen in national law, citizens may anticipate lower future pay-out levels as a result of population ageing and restrictions on government spending.

Investment or mutual funds invest clients' money in securities or money markets instruments and are sold as separate units. Several forms of funds exist, ranging from funds that invest in a particular sort of security (bonds, equity, money market instruments) to mixed funds that invest in a particular combination of such securities.

Considerable differences exist across countries in distribution channels of mutual funds. Of the largest EU countries, bank branches dominate in Germany, France and Spain with shares between 60 and 80%. In the UK and Italy, by contrast, independent agents dominate the market with shares of almost 50%. In the US, various groups of financial institutions and independent brokers compete in the mutual fund market, reflecting the segmentation of the US financial system (Walter 1998b; ECB 1999: p.17).

Overall, bond funds represented the largest group of investment funds in the EU in 1997, with 34%, followed by equity funds with 31% and money market funds with 23% (see Table A1.10 in Appendix 1). Some interesting observations can be made regarding the importance of the different types of funds across EU countries. Equity funds are the most important funds in the UK, Sweden, and the Low Countries. Bond funds are the most important in Austria, Germany and Luxembourg, and money market funds in Greece, Spain and France. In general, the split reflects differences in the investment behaviour of the other institutional investors, which to a certain extent is normal, since investment funds are also held by other institutional investors. To the extent, however, that investment funds are held by individual citizens, it reflects the perceived differences in investment behaviour: a decided preference for equity in the English-speaking countries and for fixed income in the major continental European countries. As could be noticed over recent years, this is changing rapidly, with the overall decline in long-term interest rates stimulating the growth of equity funds, mainly at the expense of money market funds.

Clearing and Settlement Agents

Growing portfolio diversification underlines the importance of safe and efficient clearance and settlement services.[9] In general,

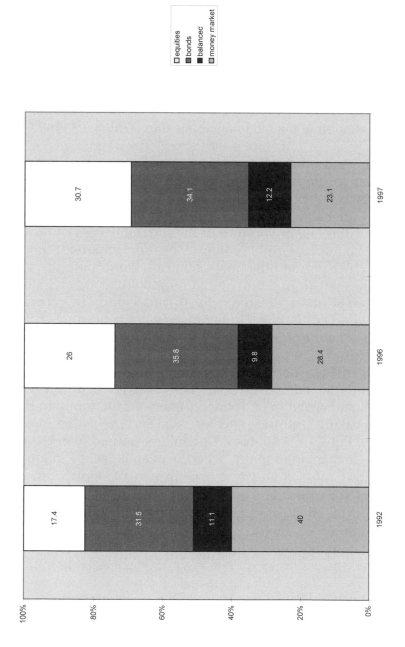

Graph 2.3 *Asset distribution of investment funds in the EU*
Source: FEFSI

the higher the clearing and settlement costs, the more investors are restrained from achieving optimum portfolios. These costs impose an explicit and implicit tax on trading, and can hinder the growth of domestic securities markets and international or cross-border trade in securities. Inefficient clearing and settlement could impede the development of a European capital market.

Clearance and settlement are services that arise from securities trading. Clearance involves the determination of what each party is due to receive. Settlement involves the actual transfer of securities from the seller to the buyer, with an offsetting payment in cash. In most cases, a national central securities depository (CSD) handles the bookkeeping-type clearance function and the securities side of the settlement, while the cash side is usually effected through the banking or payment system. In most member states, a semi-official CSD has the effective monopoly on clearance and settlement. In Germany, Deutsche Börse Clearing is structured as a cooperative, and has close links with the Bundesbank. In France, the Sicovam is owned by banks and brokers, with representatives of the principal regulators on its board.

Many CSDs also offer connected services, going from basic custodial services, such as coupon collection, redemption, tax reporting, to ancillary services such as money transfers, cash management, and redenominating or reconventioning securities. The latter services were, for example, required for changing the stock of outstanding government debt to the euro, as happened in all participating member states. Apart from the CSDs, there are also international central securities depositories (ICSDs), the best known being Cedel and Euroclear, which emerged as clearers for the Euro-bond business. They are increasingly competing for local business with the national CSDs.

Settlement of cross-border trades in the EU used to be more costly than domestic ones, but settlement with an ICSD was much cheaper than through national CSDs in bilateral links (Giddy, Saunders and Walter 1996). This raises the question of which model is most adapted for an integrated European capital market. Basic economics would seem to favour a greater centralisation of services, if European securities become sufficiently homogeneous. This has not happened so far, however, possibly due to a concern not to impinge on free competition, but most probably because of market protection in favour of local CSDs and regulatory differences.

NOTES

1. The 8 US exchanges are: NYSE, NASDAQ, AMEX, Boston, Cincinatti, Chicago, Philadelphia and the Pacific Exchange (Los Angeles and San Francisco). AMEX and NASDAQ are in the process of merging. The regional exchanges in the US do not function as a listing platform for regional firms, but as a parallel market for the big exchanges. They can attract orders thanks to lower costs.

2. The reliability of data on stock market capitalisation may be impaired by circular holdings—the cross-shareholding of listed companies. The Federation of European Stock Exchanges (1993) estimated that the degree of direct circular holdings between the 5% largest companies on a stock exchange was less than 10%. The smallest circular holding ratios were found in Dublin, London and Athens, where they seemed to be almost non-existent. Paris, Brussels and Stockholm had the largest degrees, with 15%, 22% and 26%, respectively. This may, however, have diminished recently with market restructuring and rationalisation of listings.

3. The data compilation by Salomon Brothers was continued in 1999 after an interruption of almost 1 year, meaning that 1997–1998 data was not available at the time of writing.

4. This paragraph is based upon Benzie (1992).

5. Euribor, the interbank reference rate, is calculated on the basis of quotations from 57 banks, of which 47 represent the euro markets in the participating member states and 10 are active within the euro area but with head office outside; for euro-Libor, it concerns 16 major banks active in the euro market in London. The rates flow within the corridor set by the marginal lending facility and the deposit facility of the ECB.

6. The European Commission (1997d) estimated that the cost of managing various currencies in Europe was close to 1% of GDP.

7. *The Economist*, 24 February 1996, p. 81.
8. Paolo Cecchini chaired the European Commission study group on the cost of non-Europe, which provided the intellectual support for the single market programme, see Cecchini (1988).
9. The following is based on Giddy, Saunders and Walter, 'Clearance and Settlement' (1996).

3
Market Restructuring and EMU

A key characteristic of financial markets, which are supposedly global, is the parochial nature of most of the investors. Because of exchange rate fluctuations, returns on foreign assets (whether bonds or stocks) often do not correlate with domestic returns. This implies that foreign assets should have a low beta or systematic risk and thus should form an important part of a balanced portfolio. However, all empirical studies on this issue (for two recent examples, see French and Poterba 1991; Tesar and Werner 1995) show that the degree of international diversification is small (foreign assets usually account for less than 10% of the portfolios of households and other investors, as shown below) and certainly smaller than what would be considered optimal according to the usual models of pricing risk that are otherwise dependable. It appears that even in the smaller countries, whose currencies have been tightly linked to the DEM for decades so that the exchange rate risk was minimal, investors still have a strong bias towards their own national securities.

A key issue for financial markets is thus whether investors will look at the euro area as one market or will still show a presumption in favour of their national 'home' market. Even under EMU, returns will not be perfectly correlated across industries for several reasons: cost structures differ, labour markets are still organised along national lines and a host of policies (social, fiscal, etc.) affecting profits also remain national.

But this implies that international diversification should still lead to lower overall risk and therefore should remain attractive. It is difficult to decide whether these conditions will lead to one integrated euro capital market just because the veil of different currencies has been removed.

This chapter will discuss how capital markets might be affected by EMU. Will EMU lead to a more US-style capital market? How will asset allocation patterns evolve along the different segments of capital markets? How will financial centres be affected?

A MORE MARKET-BASED SYSTEM TO EMERGE?

With the successful launch of the euro, the start of ESCB monetary policy operations and the operation of the TARGET payment system, the previously national interbank markets have been integrated straightaway into a unified euro interbank market. Outstanding public debt has been redenominated in euros, trading conventions harmonised and all EMU stock markets have started quoting in euros. This raises the expectation of a US-style capital market in Europe, with deep markets in the different segments, money, equity, bond and derivatives. This will, however, not come about so quickly. Euroland remains profoundly different from the US in two aspects:

(i) Regional differences: The terms and conditions under which enterprises finance investment and the role of intermediaries still vary considerably from country to country in the EU. This is due to deeply rooted structural differences in legal systems, development of markets and institutions, and the role of the state.
(ii) The importance of banks: Bank credit has played a much more important role than market-based forms of financing of investments by enterprises in the EU. Disintermediation, and institutionalisation of savings in pension and investment funds, is much less developed than in the US.

Because of regional differences, countries will react differently to changes in circumstances. Transmission mechanisms of monetary policy differ in the EU. In Britain, the Netherlands and Spain, short-term bank lending rates are almost fully adjusted to the central banks' weekly rates within three months; in Germany and France, on the other hand, it takes nine months to one year. The financing structure of firms differs, with considerable differences in their dependence on external funds. The attractiveness and costs of stock market listings differ, direct issues of debt on the market were until recently very difficult in several European countries, and some still are, for example, mortgage-backed securities. Tax systems differ in the treatment of distributed profits as compared to non-distributed profits and in tax credits for residents as compared to non-residents.

The dominating role of banks in the EU finds no parallel in the US. Total bank assets in the euro zone stand at three times the size of US commercial bank and savings institutions assets. This results from the segmentation of the US financial system in the 1933 Glass–Steagall Act, which separated commercial from investment banking and brokerage, and the popular mistrust against concentrated financial power, embedded in the anti-trust legislation. Although the US regime is still considered as a handicap, preventing US banks from exploiting economies of scale and scope available to foreign banks not subject to the separation, the segmentation of the US financial industry stimulated tough competition between intermediaries. It provided the environment in which capital market financing, specialisation and financial innovation emerged, creating the most competitive industry world-wide. According to Steinherr (1998: pp. 29, 39–42), 'in no other industry has the United States been as resolutely superior as in the financial industry. ... All significant innovations have come out of the US financial system.'

The competitive process between commercial banks, investment banks and brokers in the US stimulated a process of disintermediation and securitisation. Caps on short-term bank deposits led to the emergence of higher yielding money market mutual funds. Banks responded by transforming liabilities into negotiable certificates of deposits, on which interest could be paid without restriction. In order to get a share of the profitable loan market, investment banks stimulated corporations in securitising their loans. As a result, the balance sheets of banks became fully disintermediated and securitised, and with this relationship banking disappeared. The growth of a deep and liquid money and capital market had deprived relationship of its implicit insurance value, and made valuations more important. The key principle of transparency, that underlies US financial, securities and accounting law, emerged.

In Europe, the universal banking system has remained dominant. Although most Latin European countries followed the US-model separation between investment banking and commercial lending until the late 1980s, the universal banking model was taken as the model in the EU's financial market liberalisation of the single market programme. There was no incentive for banks to securitise debt, and capital markets were underdeveloped. Furthermore, the regulatory framework for direct issues on capital markets left much to be desired (see below). For example, corporate bonds were until recently discouraged in Germany through very strict emission criteria, that is with the obligation to issue only in domestic currency on the local market, and unfavourable tax treatment. Governments wished to keep close control of the local debt securities market for proper purposes.

These differences in the role of financial intermediaries are reflected in the financing structure of the economy. Liabilities of non-financial companies with banks differ from 33% in the US, 50% in the UK to about 80% in most continental European countries (BIS).

Data on the importance of securities as compared to banking markets confirm the asymmetry between the American and European systems. US bond markets and equity are twice the size of their EU counterparts. EU commercial bank assets, on the other hand, dwarf the assets of US commercial banks (see Table 3.1).

Another outcome of the segmentation of the US financial system is the strength of institutional investors. Pension and investment funds are much more important players in the US

Table 3.1   *Amounts of bonds outstanding, total stock market capitalisation and bank assets*

1997	Bond markets (ECU bn)	% GDP	Equity markets (ECU bn)	% GDP	Commercial bank assets (ECU bn)	% GDP
EU 11	6,174	109.3	2,707	47.9	11,583	212.3
EU 15	7,903	111.6	4,946	69.9	13,265	195.6
US	12,430	206.4	9,619	159.7	3,585	62.5

Sources: BIS, FESE, OECD; Bank data are 1996; US stock market data refer to NYSE and NASDAQ.

than in the EU (see Graph 3.1). This is, however, related not only to the regulatory framework for financial markets, but even more to the reach of the welfare state and the design of social security systems. Total state financing (pay-as-you-go) and high replacement ratios in retirement systems explain the limited role of pension funds in many EU countries. Although 'institutionalised' saving in investment funds has also started to grow rapidly in Europe, it is, unlike in the US, largely inter-mediated by the banks. Banks have thus internalised the dis-intermediation process.

Taken together, segments that might form the composing elements of a more market-based system exist but they are spread in each case over different EU countries, and are on an aggregate basis small as compared to the equivalent US segment. The following markets are well developed in the following countries:

- Pension funds: UK, Netherlands, Ireland
- Investment funds: France, Spain, Luxembourg
- Mortgage bonds: Germany, Denmark, Sweden
- Corporate bonds: France, UK

It is therefore difficult to say at this moment whether a more market-based system will emerge in Europe. The strength of the bank system will have a dampening effect on the development of a more market-based system. Also many elements in the reg-ulatory framework will need to be adapted. Issuing bonds directly on to the market requires a different attitude from getting a loan from the bank. It requires more transparency,

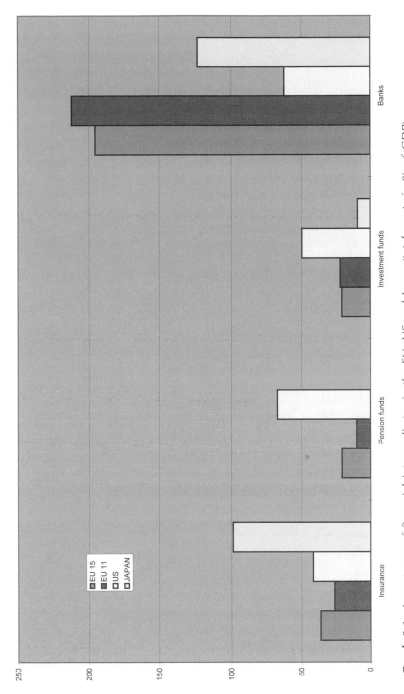

Graph 3.1 Importance of financial intermediaries in the EU, US and Japan (total assets in % of GDP)
Sources: CEA, FESE, FIBV, OECD

market-based accounting standards, rating services—elements that will not emerge overnight.

This book is about capital markets, and does not discuss other sectors of banking where European banks are more competitive than their US counterparts. Retail banking, for example, is more developed in the EU than in the US, as a result of fierce competition between banks to attract depositors and regulatory impediments in the US. However, the competitive advantage of the US in investment banking raises the question whether the benefits of a euro capital market might not go to the well-established US investment banks. European banks are scarce in the rankings of M&A advisers, for example, which are dominated by institutions of US origin, even for European deals. Only two European banks, the US investment banking offshoots of the Swiss banks, were part of the 1998 world-wide top ten; five in the European top ten. This can lead to ironic situations, as was the case in the takeover battle of the Belgian Générale Bank between the Fortis Group and ABN–AMRO, where both sides were advised by US investment banks. The same applies in other segments of investment banking, such as the securities underwriting business and asset management. European banks, with the exception of the two big Swiss banks, have been notorious for their failure to develop global investment banking operations so far. The years to come will show whether they will succeed in Europe, and face the competition of their US counterparts.

ASSET ALLOCATION IN EMU

The parameters for portfolio diversification changed with EMU. The introduction of the euro eliminates currency-matching rules as a barrier to cross-border investments for insurance companies, but the elimination of currency risks and the integration of bond markets might also reduce the benefits of cross-country diversification, since markets are more correlated.[1] Two aspects therefore need to be distinguished: the impact of EMU on the regulatory barriers for portfolio diversification and the implications for optimal asset allocation.

From a regulatory point of view, the most important changes should happen in the fixed interest portfolio of insurance companies. EU-licensed insurance companies are subject to an 80% currency-matching rule, meaning that at least 80% of the currency denomination of the assets has to match those of the liabilities. EMU should allow these companies to spread their assets over a much larger currency area, since EMU currencies are irrevocably fixed and national currencies are considered as subdivisions of the euro.[2] Moreover, the redenomination of national debt into euros by all participating member states and the changeover of equity markets to the euro turns the asset side of their balance sheets predominantly into euros. As indicated earlier, harmonised rules for pension funds do not exist in the EU. Changes for pension fund investment as a direct result of EMU are less important, however, since the Netherlands and the UK, which represent 74% of pension fund assets in the EU (1996), have no meaningful quantitative restrictions on pension fund investment (with the exception of the Dutch civil servant pension fund ABP). The effect on pension funds should be mainly indirect.

Traditionally, continental European institutional investors have invested massively in domestic government debt (see Tables 2.5 and 2.6). The replacement of the domestic by a euro currency-matching rule allows them to rebalance into debt securities of other EMU member states issued in euros. From a prudential point of view, they should even be encouraged to spread their investments. But to what extent will this happen? Continental European institutional investors do not have the reputation of being very active investors. EMU further increases competition, and divergence in yields based on the fiscal position of the different EMU members could be an incentive for insurers to diversify into debt securities of other member states.

The strongest reason for institutional investors to diversify their holdings is that their performance will be measured against a euro-area benchmark index for stocks and bonds. Several indexes have been developed by index providers, such as the FTSE' Europtop, the Dow Jones' Stoxx or the MSCI Europe for the equity markets, and the Reuters' Govtop Euro

Treasury Indexes, Barclays' Capital Euro Government Bond Indices or Merrill Lynch EMU Broad Market index for government bonds. Bond indexes are based on the euro zone, whereas equity indexes often distinguish between the euro zone and the wider Europe. The country weights in the Barclays' Capital Euro Government Bond Index are represented in Table 3.2, compared with the share of government debt outstanding as part of the total euro zone government debt. For some countries, such as France and Italy, the shares of outstanding debt differ importantly from their share in the government bond index, which could have an impact on the spreads.

A sector spread of the equity index DJ Euro Stoxx 50 is represented in Graph 3.2. Profound differences exist in presence in the index depending on the nationality of firms, to the extent that this principle is still relevant. Companies which are incorporated in Germany, France and the Netherlands have weights of, respectively, 29.5, 22.7 and 23.3%, whereas countries such as Austria and Luxembourg are not represented at all.

Assumptions were made on the implications for the different government bond markets of portfolio rescheduling by institutional investors, based on the importance of the different bond markets and on ownership structure. According to one estimate, the French government bond market could experience a substantial outflow, because of the high proportion of

Table 3.2 Shares of EMU states in outstanding debt and shares in a Euro-bond index

	Barclays' Capital Euro Government Bond Index	Euro government bond market share
Germany	23.8	23
Italy	22.3	32
France	22.1	17
Spain	8.7	6
Netherlands	8.5	7
Belgium	8	8
Austria	2.7	3
Finland	1.9	1
Portugal	1	2
Ireland	1	1
Total	100	100

Source: Barclay Capital, BIS (1998).

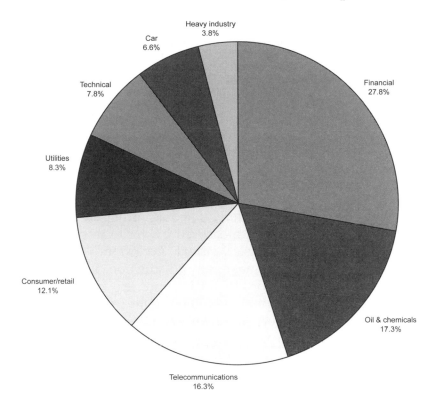

Graph 3.2 *Euro Stoxx 50 index according to sector*
Source: Euro Stoxx

French debt held by French institutional investors. The Italian market, in contrast, would gain significantly, for the opposite reason (Brookes 1998). On the equity side, asset allocation should move from country-based towards EU-wide sector-oriented investment policies.

The issue of rebalancing portfolios applies equally to the banking sector, but mainly on prudential grounds. It has been proposed (see e.g., Bishop 1991) that once the third stage of EMU starts, the prudential rules for the banking system should be changed to take into account the increased risk of public debt that comes once the ECB takes over monetary policy. The argument is that once the third stage has started, national governments lose the power to print money. Banks, especially in some highly indebted countries, have an important part of their assets invested in government debt. High exposure of the financial sector to the public sector links the fate of both, which may be particularly destabilising in times of financial instability. Banks in EU countries with the highest debt ratios, such as Belgium, Greece and Italy, also have the highest exposures to government and low ROA ratios (Arnold 1998). In view of the EU's directive limiting large exposures, the disappearance of currency risk, and macro-economic stability, they should even be required to spread their investments in government paper of different EMU member states. Furthermore, weightings of government debt could be differentiated according to the creditworthiness of the borrower, measured by, for example, credit ratings. But neither the Basle Capital Accord nor the EU's solvency ratios directive make any distinction in the risk weighting of public debt for all OECD countries, and the large exposures directive exempts government debt from its rules.

The sharp increase in correlation between the euro-zone bond markets could also be an argument for diversification into other less correlated markets. According to the Markowitz mean-variance efficiency theory, diversification of managed assets leads to diminished risk, without implying any decline in expected returns. In addition, the lower the degree of correlation among the assets managed, the more effective is the diversification in reducing the risk return. Merrill Lynch (1999) compares the risk return trade-off of portfolios resulting from different combinations between Spanish and German bonds. Diversification in 1995 between the two countries led to a considerable increase in return for a given level of risk. By 1998, the increase in correlation between the two countries meant that the benefits from diversification were much lower, entailing an additional risk for the same level of return. Diversification benefits are thus reduced in the EMU zone, which might lead investors to search for less correlated markets. However, as discussed above, institutional investors are not internationally diversified and cross-country diversification has been limited so far.

BOND MARKETS IN THE EURO ZONE

Prospects for the Sovereign Debt Market

Since the start of EMU, there has been one EMU-wide euro government bond market. New issues of government debt are issued in euros and almost all outstanding debt has been redenominated in euros and reconventioned, thus creating the world's second largest government bond market with a single market standard. Such an integrated public debt market eases issuing and reduces government financing costs. Governments no longer need to cover the whole maturity spectrum and are faced with a more liquid and competitive market.

The euro government bond market does not have one central debtor, however, and thus remains fundamentally different from the US market. Europe will not have a single centre with fiscal powers in the foreseeable future, and fiscal policy-making continues to fall within the domain of the member states. The ECB sets the common money market interest rate, but the judgement of the creditworthiness of the different EU states and regions rests with the market. From a theoretical point of view, the euro area is unique in that the risk-free rate of interest that is posted in most finance models does not exist. Issues by governments and well-capitalised international institutions, such as the European Investment Bank, are almost risk free, but only almost.

An important indicator of the momentum towards EMU was the convergence of yields on long-term debt of the group of the most likely EMU countries against the benchmark of the German Bunds (Graph 3.3). Yields of the southern European countries fell dramatically from spreads of several hundred basis points to some 20 basis points. At certain times, government debt was priced more on the basis of the political commitment of the government wanting to join EMU than on the basis of present and prospective fiscal performance. UK Treasury gilts, for example, were priced considerably higher than Spanish bonos, although the UK fiscal performance was no worse than Spain's. The difference between the UK and Italy is even more

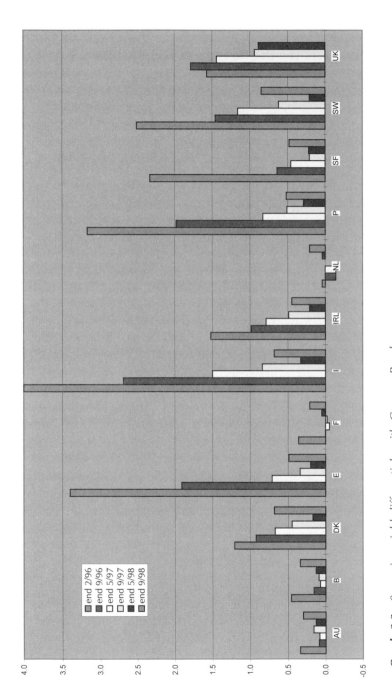

Graph 3.3 Sovereign yield differentials with German Bunds

pronounced. This raises the question whether the market expects that EMU implies some common responsibility for sovereign debt, notwithstanding the no-bail-out clause of the Maastricht Treaty.

How will spreads in bond yields evolve in EMU? Different elements can be taken into consideration. A first possibility is to look at the interest rate spreads on sovereign paper denominated in the same currency, such as DEM, before EMU. As can be seen from Table 3.3, the spreads were very low, suggesting that the market worried more about currency risk than about fiscal risk. However, a problem with foreign currency sovereign paper spreads is that they usually constitute only a small proportion of overall public debt. The market might thus assume that even if a country got into trouble, it might still be willing and able to fully service its foreign debt because it is so small relative to the total. This might explain why countries that had a relatively high proportion of their overall debt denominated in foreign currency (pre-EMU, of course), such as Ireland and Finland, had relatively low ratings on their foreign currency debt.

Table 3.3 *Long-term foreign currency sovereign credit ratings in the EU and yield differentials on Euro-DEM bonds (in basis points, September 1997)*

Country	Moody's	Standard & Poor's	Euro-DEM bond spread (Sept. '97)	Domestic currency DEM spread (end Sept. '97)	Debt/ GDP ratio	Existence of excessive deficit (as defined in EU Treaty)
Germany	Aaa	AAA			61.8	Yes
France	Aaa	AAA		−2	57.3	Yes
Austria	Aaa	AAA	16	16	66.1	Yes
Neth.	Aaa	AAA		0	73.4	No
Belgium	Aa1	AA+	21	9	124.7	Yes
Ireland	Aa1	AA	19	49	65.8	No
Denmark	Aa1	AA+	21	45	67.0	No
Finland	Aa1	AA−	19	21	59.0	No
UK	Aaa	AAA		94	52.9	Yes
Sweden	Aa3	AA+	21	62	77.4	Yes
Spain	Aa2	AA	23	34	68.1	Yes
Italy	Aa3	AA	23	84	123.2	Yes
Portugal	Aa3	AA−		51	62.5	Yes
Greece	Baa1	BBB−			109.3	Yes

A second element is to take the ratings of the different agencies (Fitch–IBCA, Moody's, Standard & Poor's) into consideration. The point of reference pre-EMU was the *foreign currency* rating, which has become the standard in EMU. In September 1997, of all EU countries, Austria, France, Germany, Luxembourg, the Netherlands and the UK received the highest rating. Finland and Ireland were rated in the second or third class, although both countries were at the time of the rating outside the Maastricht excessive deficit procedure, whereas Germany, France and the UK had an excessive deficit in 1997. This compared with triple A ratings which all EU countries except Greece got on local currency debt.

At the start of EMU, considerations for fixing the ratings changed, leading to some important modifications in the foreign currency ratings from pre-EMU. The fiscal criteria (deficit, debt and debt structure) for assessing sovereign creditworthiness became more important than the external criteria (balance of payments, savings rate). Furthermore, the competitive element came into play much more than before, as investors had a choice of sovereign paper in their own currency of 11 member states. On the eve of EMU, Fitch–IBCA downgraded Belgium from 'AA+' to 'AA−', at the same level as Italy, because of dependence on short-term debt and its high debt levels, increasing the risk of a liquidity crisis. But the agency upgraded Finland and Ireland to 'AAA', and Portugal to 'AA', reflecting successful fiscal consolidation (Table 3.4).[3]

A third more far-away example of the degree of divergence is the credit spreads on debt issued by the Canadian provinces, some of which are known to be strongly attached to their identity. It suggests that spreads might amount to about 50 basis points for 10-year bonds, a slight increase as compared to the spreads which could be noticed at the start of EMU. But it again indicates that the market does not extract a very high risk premium for differences in fiscal performance, since Canadian provinces with a low credit rating have low spreads with the best performing ones. It could be argued that spreads on euro public securities would be bigger in Europe, however, since taxes are higher in Europe (and room for tax increases is limited), and there is a 'no bail-out' clause in the EU Treaty. In

Table 3.4   *Sovereign credit ratings in the euro zone (early 1999)*

	Moody's	S&P	Fitch–IBCA
Germany	Aaa	AAA	AAA
France	Aaa	AAA	AAA
Luxembourg	Aaa	AAA	AAA
Netherlands	Aaa	AAA	AAA
Austria	Aaa	AAA	AAA
Belgium	Aa1	AA+	AA–
Ireland	Aa1	AA+	AAA
Finland	Aa1	AA	AAA
Spain	Aa2	AA+	AA
Portugal	Aa3	AA–	AA
Italy	Aa3	AA	AA–

Canada, on the other hand, there is some form of constructive ambiguity in the guarantee of provincial debt.[4]

The yield differentials during the September 1998 financial crisis could be an indication of the highest spreads that will exist within EMU. At the end of September 1998, spreads with German Bunds differed from 20 basis points for France and the Netherlands to 50 for Portugal and Spain and 68 for Italy. In any event, differences of hundreds of basis points, as existed in the past, should be definitively over within EMU.

The rating of government debt has to be seen in the perspective of the zero risk weighting which these instruments enjoy in the EU's solvency ratios directive. Hence, even if ratings for government paper do vary within the euro zone, and in certain cases fall even lower than ratings for commercial paper, governments can still be sure of finding a wide market.

A second question which has been often debated in the run-up to EMU is what country will provide the benchmark. It has been argued that the German Bunds might lose their benchmark status in EMU to France because French government bonds cover the maturity spectrum more evenly, and thus provide sufficient liquidity in all segments of the market. Second, French products are more marketable. German debt is more widely dispersed over central and local government and in different products. Third, the French markets are supported by a transparent and liquid market for repurchase agreements, while the bulk of DEM repo trading was, until recently, located in London.

It is unlikely, however, that bonds of only one country will continue to constitute the euro-area benchmark. Benchmarks might differ along the maturity spectrum, with French debt providing the benchmark for the medium term debt and Germany for the long term. A euro government bond index might also be created similar to the ECU-based index that exists today with the 'best to deliver' approach. Such an index might, but not necessarily, include only triple-A-rated government bonds. The experience with the ECU-based index has shown that differences of a few dozen basis points are not an obstacle to constructing such an index.

The advent of EMU led to strong cooperation between EU governments on the redenomination and reconventioning of existing debt and on common market conventions for new debt. An ad hoc Working Party (the Brouhns Committee) was constituted in the Monetary Committee and agreed in its report that the bottom-up method, as advised by the Commission's Giovannini Group (European Commission 1997e), was to be followed for redenominating existing debt.[5] According to this approach, individual holdings were converted into euros at fixed conversion rates, rounded up to the nearest cent.[6] This compared to the top-down approach, whereby a bond is converted into new bonds with round nominal values in euros, leading to compensatory payments to account for the differences. The ad hoc Working Party harmonised most market conventions for *new* debt issues (Treasury bills and bonds), such as the actual/actual day count convention for accrued interest calculation of bonds (i.e. based on the actual number of days over which the interest is accrued and the actual number of days in the year) and the actual/360-day count basis for bills, the quotation basis (prices with decimals) and the business days.[7] They have been followed in all member states from 1 January 1999 onwards, with the exception of Denmark and Sweden, where the issue was not yet settled at the time of writing. Harmonised market conventions allow for easy comparisons of bond yields, thus stimulating market integration. Some differences remain, however, on coupon frequency and settlement dates, particularly for old *outstanding* debt issues.[8]

More fine-tuning between the member states on the timing, size and maturity of debt issues should result automatically from an integrated Euro-bond market. It is evident that, within the euro zone, member states will closely watch each others' debt emission programmes. Member states will avoid tapping the market jointly in the same period. Variations will be pursued in the size, techniques and maturity of emissions, which should reduce the cost of issues and public finance management, and finally benefit the taxpayers.

A Corporate Bond Market to Emerge?

The harmonisation of market conventions will also apply to new private debt issues in the euro zone, which should be a first element facilitating its growth. Overall, a significant increase is expected in demand for corporate debt, as a result of strict limitations on public finance in the Stability Pact, credit diversification by investors and stronger competition among intermediaries.

Traditionally, corporate debt markets have been poorly developed in Europe. The stock of bonds issued by non-financial companies in the EMU 11 was just $160bn as of the end of February 1998, as compared to over $1 trillion in the US (Brookes and Winkelmann 1998). Many reasons could be put forward, but the lack of a liquid market is perhaps one of the most important. Monetary union, but also the competitive process it will trigger, will bring change. Corporates will be faced with a more mature financial market, which will allow a wider choice of different financing instruments. Banks will look for more profitable activities, such as acting as lead managers for bond issues. Demand from institutional investors for more diversified portfolios could also contribute to the growth of the commercial paper market.

Before, corporate borrowing in the euro-zone countries occurred for 80% or more through banks. Only France had a significant corporate debt market. In the US, on the contrary, corporates borrow more through bond issuance than from banks. This explains the profound difference in the distribution of bonds over the rating spectrum between the US and the EU. In the euro zone, 70% of the issuance was rated Aa2 (AA) before EMU, according to Moody's, compared to 30% for the US. This so-called 'credit gap' is expected to narrow in EMU (Bank of England 1998: Issue No. 9).

Several elements should contribute to the development of corporate debt markets in Europe. Limited prospects for the government debt market as a result of the Stability and Growth Pact and historically low yields of government debt should lead to more demand for higher yielding private debt. Corporate issuers will no longer be constrained by the credit ratings of their own government, with a possibility for higher credit ratings on private paper than some euro-zone governments. Issuing cost should fall as a result of a deeper and more liquid euro-market and stronger competition between market intermediaries.

Mortgage Loan Markets

National idiosyncrasies at the retail level can have their implications at the wholesale level, but they might not be directly affected by EMU. A good example in this case is the European mortgage loan markets, which demonstrate a wide diversity in mortgage contracts and refinancing methods. At the retail level, the interest rate can be variable or fixed over a long term. At the wholesale level, mortgage loans can be refinanced through short-term deposits or through long-term bonds and mortgage-backed securities. In the past, these differences coincided with country-specific patterns, exemplified by the building societies in the UK at one extreme, using variable rates financed by short-term deposits, and by the *Hypothekenbanken* in Germany, on the other, using fixed rates financed by long-term *Pfandbriefe*.

A reason for the differences was the much higher level and variability of inflation in the UK during the 1970s and 1980s. The real rate paid by borrowers would have been extremely variable if nominal interest rates on mortgage loans had been fixed for 5–10 years as is customary in Germany. More recently, variable rates have also been offered in Germany so that the differences are not as stark as before. Considerable differences continue, however, and regulatory barriers prevent the emergence of a truly integrated market. These relate to differences in securities, consumer protection, bankruptcy and tax legislation.

Mortgage lending is one of the activities that can be exercised on a cross-border basis, according to the second banking directive, and is subject to home country supervision only. Loopholes in the latter directive, such as the general good clause, and remaining differences in tax, securities and property legislation, however, have proven to be serious barriers to the cross-border provision of mortgage services, leaving host country authorities with considerable scope to exercise control, or making cross-border business uninteresting. Sometimes long-term refinancing through mortgage bonds was not possible in the host country, since the bankruptcy legislation, that is determined by the place of the estate for which a loan is provided, did not give lenders as much security as in their home country. Hence it follows that certain, possibly competitive, forms of mortgage lending have not yet sufficiently spread at a European-wide level. From a capital markets perspective, it implies that such long-term private debt instruments have not yet further developed in Europe.

As of today, the development of mortgage loan markets differs markedly in the EU (see Table 3.5). They are very developed in the UK and Denmark, but almost non-existent in Austria and Italy. The way this affects capital markets differs even more. A liquid mortgage bond market exists only in Denmark, Germany and Sweden. Outstanding mortgage bonds in Denmark almost equal GDP. In Germany, the share of mortgage bonds looks limited, but mortgage bonds are only a quarter of the total *Pfandbriefe* outstanding, the biggest part of which is composed of public sector bonds. At EU level, total mortgage bonds and mortgage-backed securities outstanding represent only 15% of the total of outstanding mortgage loans (for the EU 11 it is 11%). Mortgage-backed securities are a very tiny part of the latter category, and represent only

Table 3.5   *Total volume of mortgage loans and mortgage bonds outstanding (1997)*

ECU bn	Total volume of mortgage loans outstanding	% of GDP	Mortgage bonds outstanding	Bonds as % of loans (c/a)
B	53.7	24.9	1.0	1.8
DK	123.5	85.7	134.6	109.0
DE	1128.8	58.9	207.6	18.4
EL	6.2	6.0		
E	145.7	30.2	8.3	5.7
F	251.0	20.0	2.2	0.9
I	111.4	11.1		
IRL	20.4	33.3		
L	3.6	26.0		
NL	264.0	82.3	2.5	1.0
AU	9.4	5.1	4.9	52.2
P	27.9	31.3	0.1	0.4
SF	30.9	29.7	1.3	4.1
SW	115.6	54.4	81.4	70.4
UK	647.2	66.7	NA	
EU11	2046.7	36.2	227.9	11.1
EU15	2939.1	41.5	443.9	15.1
US			2059.3	

Note: For Greece, France, Finland and the UK, the data refer to residential mortgage loans only; mortgage bonds include mortgage bonds and mortgage-backed securities; US data are USD federal agency mortgage bonds and non-agency mortgage securities.
Source: European Mortgage Federation (1998) and Salomon Smith Banney (1999).

2% of total mortgage bonds outstanding.[9] Total mortgage bonds outstanding corresponds to 6% of GDP in the EU (or 4% for EU 11), 95% of which is represented by Denmark, Germany and Sweden, as compared to 35% in the US, where mortgage-backed securities form an important part of capital markets.

Although some remaining structural and regulatory barriers are being reduced by monetary union, this will not happen overnight. The unification of monetary policy, the disappearance of currency risk and the classification of securities instruments at EU level (in the rules on collateral for monetary policy operations of the ECB) should provide host country authorities with less scope for additional control. The impetus that has recently been given to harmonising withholding tax could remove another important barrier. Given the price stability objective of the ECB and the expected stable short-term interest rate environment, the incidence of fixed-rate long-term mortgage loans may increase under EMU, and with it long-term refinancing, provided other elements in the regulatory framework are addressed.

EQUITY AND DERIVATIVES MARKETS

The perspective of EMU and the disappearance of national currencies has brought about sea changes in organised markets. An obvious victim of EMU is derivative exchanges, but restructuring is also affecting stock markets. Both are exploring the possibilities of increased cooperation. In derivative markets, the agreement between the German DTB and the Swiss SOFFEX to form EUREX set the tune for a series of cooperation agreements between exchanges. EUREX gives its members access to one common trading platform, without physically merging their floors. In other cases, smaller derivative exchanges have merged with the local stock markets to form a single legal entity.

Also in equity markets, the trend towards agglomeration has grown. In the past, several initiatives to create more cooperation between European exchanges failed, and competition prevailed (Lee 1998: pp. 68–73). In the 1985 single market white paper, the Commission said more integration among European stock exchanges would stimulate their competitiveness. An initiative to interlink exchanges to create a Community-wide trading system for securities of international interest would serve that objective. However, several steps undertaken in this direction by the European federation of stock exchanges failed. In 1990, the EU 12 stock exchanges created Euroquote, which would have linked the different exchanges in a common trading platform—virtually electronically creating one exchange—but the initiative never got off the ground. In September 1995, the EU stock exchanges created Eurolist, to offer joint listings on several exchanges to European blue chip companies, requiring an amendment to the listing particulars directive (directive 94/18/EC). This initiative too was quietly abandoned in the autumn of 1997.

It is only the perspective of EMU which brought real change, and dramatically altered things, culminating in the agreement between the Frankfurt and London stock exchanges in July 1998. The cooperation agreement between the Swedish and Danish stock exchanges could be considered as a precursor to this agreement, which could finally lead to the creation of several larger exchange groupings. The Frankfurt–London agreement was later joined by the other major continental European exchanges, but it was unclear at the time of writing how far market integration would reach. Phase 1 of the alliance, a common access package, providing dual membership and a single point of liquidity for equities, applied from its start on 4 January 1999 only to the two initiators of the alliance. Both exchanges are to discourage dual-listings of their members in order to concentrate liquidity on the home market. It is only in the course of 1999 that other exchanges will formally join and that harmonised listing rules and regulations will be established, probably leading to a joint company. A single trading system, with one set of listing rules and regulations, will only be addressed at a later stage, but the end goal is to create one operational market.

The biggest problem in cooperation among exchanges, the governance of the merged entity, often seems the most simple, at least to an outsider. European exchanges differ markedly in their governance structure, going from cooperatives with equal or differentiated voting power of members to plcs that are themselves listed, whereby ownership differs from exchange membership. A trend towards demutualisation is, however, clearly under way, stimulated by market trading automation. Exchanges organised as mutuals have often been the most reluctant to adopt automated trading technology, because of vested interest, and thus also to implement remote membership. Competitive pressures can be expected to drive demutualisation further.

On the whole, cooperation and competition will continue to coincide between exchanges in a first phase. The cooperation agreements which have been announced with much fanfare are still limited in scope, and the future will have to show whether the ambitions of a single platform will be met, as competition might again intensify. What is certain is that trades will be further reoriented towards the domestic or home country exchange, as a result of the possibilities created by the ISD and the objectives of the cooperation agreements, and that foreign listings within the EU will be reduced. It is only in the longer run, as other barriers disappear and the nationality of firms becomes less clear, or more European, that some exchanges might totally disappear. Nevertheless, the success of the new exchanges for small- and medium-sized or emerging companies, such as the Euro Nouveau Marché and EASDAQ, shows that it is difficult to predict what the market will look like in a decade. The evolution in the cost of technology for trading systems should be kept in mind as an important element determining the competitive environment for stock exchanges. Exchanges could also become more functional, sector or size driven, with nationality or geography becoming less and less of an issue.

SECURITIES CLEARING AND SETTLEMENT BODIES

Related to changes in asset allocation, integration of bond markets and equity markets, a slow but definite restructuring can be expected in the securities clearing and settlement business. International clearing and securities depositories (ICSDs) will start to compete more on the national markets, whereas the central securities depositories (CSDs) will expand their services at European level. A consolidation in the number of depositories is, however, expected, since there is a redundancy of systems. On the other hand, cross-border services are expected to grow, with a strong increase in cross-border investments in Europe. Increased competition might also lead to new market configurations. To prepare this transition process, the CSDs have created the European Central Securities Depositories Association (ECSDA), which aims to develop and improve the links between them and to compete with the ICSDs.

Regarding links with the execution of the euro monetary policy, CSDs have set the objective of allowing their clients to settle and hold all European securities on the same terms as domestic securities, without additional risk or cost penalties, and wherever they choose to settle (the 'eurolinks' project). It should give banks a single point of entry for financial market operations while allowing intraday cross-border use of collateral and joint custody service levels. The Eurolinks' objective is proceeding, but not all links of the matrix have been established yet. An important number of links still needed to be implemented in 1999.

In a recent study, the ECB assessed the conformity of securities settlements systems' standards in the EU (29 September 1998). The objective was to ensure that the European System of Central Banks credit operations are processed through securities settlement systems which will: (i) prevent the national central banks from bearing inappropriate risks when conducting monetary policy operations and in providing intraday credit to TARGET participants; and (ii) ensure the same level of safety for all national central banks' operations settled in different ways throughout the European Union. The report contains the list of those eligible securities settlement systems which qualify for involvement in ESCB monetary policy and intraday credit operations. A separate assessment concerning links between securities settlement systems is currently under way. The results of the assessment of the 29 securities settlement systems show that all of them could be considered to be eligible for use in ESCB credit operations, albeit on different grounds.

FINANCIAL CENTRES

The prospect of EMU, the liberalisation of capital markets and technological progress have sharpened competition between financial centres in Europe. EMU should, however, not necessarily lead to a reduction of financial centres in Europe, as the factors for the development of financial centres will be eased, but to a rationalisation process leading to more regional specialisation. The US structure of financial centres might thereby be an indication of how the European scene will evolve.

The term 'financial centre' covers fairly distinct entities. At the two extremes, it can refer to the large *on-shore* international financial centres, such as New York, London or Tokyo, or to the smaller *off-shore* tax havens, such as Bermuda, the Caymans or the Channel Islands. In between is a rich myriad of financial centres with distinct competitive strengths. Europe harbours several financial centres of differing size, importance and specialisation.

In the past, financial centres emerged in centres of international trade. Florence, the first international financial centre, acquired its pre-eminent position in the fourteenth–fifteenth centuries on the basis of the surpluses generated by activities in international trade. The capital surpluses were, however, not a sufficient condition. A surplus required a successful intermediation process to identify investment opportunities. Proximity to the sources of capital and production remained important until telecommunications and information technology allowed the emergence of off-shore financial centres.

Several factors determine the attractiveness of a financial centre. Their relative importance and combination will differ from one centre to another. Determining factors for international financial centres are:

- Localisation: proximity to clients, customers and markets
- Human capital: know-how and creativity of labour force, international orientation
- Financial market: existence of a well-functioning and liquid capital market, exchanges
- Political and macro-economic stability, reputation
- Regulation: financial market regulation, secrecy, taxation; enforcement
- Infrastructure: real estate, communications, technology, clearance and settlement
- Commercial base: link with international commerce

EMU should directly contribute to the development of financial centres, as a more mature capital market is expected to emerge. More indirectly, macro-economic stability will be enhanced and the infrastructural framework for clearance and settlement eased. But it could also hamper further growth of financial centres that have developed as tax havens, such as Luxembourg, since more tax harmonisation is expected to result from EMU.

Today, the status of international financial centre is in heavy demand, and more countries and places are trying to attain it than there are positions available. Financial centres have started to compete as corporate entities. Efficiency is becoming more important as regulatory advantages are levelled out. Some centres specialise in specific financial services activities, as they cannot cover the whole spectrum of financial centre activities.

Big centres, such as Frankfurt and Paris, have over the last few years invested large amounts to compete with the established players, whereas new small off-shore centres, such as Dublin, Madeira or the Canary Islands, are trying to put themselves on the map. Frankfurt launched the 'Finanzplatz Deutschland' project, which encompasses promotion of the stock exchange as a financing vehicle, modernisation of capital markets (e.g. international acceptance of *Pfandbriefe*, liquidity of public debt markets), adaptation of securities law and international roadshows. Paris started 'Paris Europlace' to promote the city as an international financial centre. Both places organise a big annual event, in which all leading local personalities participate.

The City of London, in an attempt not to lose its competitive edge as a result of the UK's non-participation in the first wave of EMU, started a campaign in early 1998 to underscore its readiness for the euro. Key City figures led a series of international roadshows to the main financial centres under the slogan 'London: Ready for the Euro'. Colourful episodes of the rivalry between these financial centres in the run-up to EMU occurred in the domain of the stock exchanges, with the London and Frankfurt futures exchanges fighting for market share while their stock exchanges are joining forces to create an integrated listing platform for locally quoted companies.

Each financial centre activity has its own characteristics and locational attributes. Five groups of activities could be distinguished:

- International lending and interbank dealing: interbank lending, loan syndication, project finance
- Capital market activities: issuing and underwriting of securities (equity, bonds), trading, research and analysis
- Corporate finance: M&A advice, recapitalisations, privatisations
- Investment management and investor services: asset management, private banking
- Clearing and settlement

Some financial centre activities are highly mobile and can be carried out anywhere, others require bundling with other services or are subject to scale economies. They could be subdivided into *centrifugal or supply-oriented* and *centripetal or demand-oriented* (Walter 1998a). Centrifugal activities can be carried out in remote locations to take advantage of lower labour, real estate costs or other production considerations. Examples of centrifugal activities are: transactions processing, brokerage, private banking, retail banking, asset management. Centripetal activities are driven by proximity and economies of agglomeration. They are risk management, corporate advisory services, securities underwriting, trading and sales, loan structuring and syndication, foreign exchange and money market dealing.

Whereas centripetal forces dominated in the financial services industry in the past, increased competition and modern technology allow centrifugal forces to have a greater impact. Soaring operational costs in the larger financial centres are supporting the trend to unbundle activities in different components and to separate non-core services to be carried out in other locations, or to be outsourced. As a result of these developments, the threshold between centrifugal and centripetal forces has recently moved 'significantly to the periphery' (Walter 1998a). Further rationalisation in the financial services industry can be expected, benefiting remote financial centres, which can offer a good infrastructure, qualified labour and an attractive tax and regulatory environment. Prime candidates for relocation are back-office operations and data processing. Such activities could even be pooled among a number of firms to bring down costs, which requires high-capacity facilities.

Within Europe, the position of Frankfurt, as headquarters of the ECB, will rise, but it is unlikely that a single dominant financial centre will quickly emerge, because of the large degree of decentralisation in the execution of monetary policy and the remaining regulatory and fiscal idiosyncrasies that keep certain markets segmented. In the longer run, the US structure of financial centres might be an indication of how the European scene will evolve. Apart from New York, there are dispersed asset management centres (Boston, Chicago, Philadelphia, Stanford, San Francisco). Some of these centres focus on particular financial instruments (futures in Chicago) or industries (high-tech in San Francisco) that have their roots in region-specific strengths.

An example of regulatory idiosyncrasy that is important to the competitive position of financial centres is the regulation of primary dealers in sovereign debt. So far member states have wished to maintain discretion in the regulation of primary dealers for obvious reasons. Primary dealer rules do not fall within the scope of the investment services directive and were deliberately kept outside the discussions of the Brouhns Committee on the coordination of public debt management in the EU, referred to above. Non-harmonisation of primary dealer rules and the non-application of the single licence in this area require banks to maintain subsidiaries in different EU financial centres and to forgo scale economies. In the long run, however, it is likely that this situation will not be sustainable, as some smaller countries have already acknowledged. Belgium, for example, reformed its primary dealer rules and does not require banks to have a permanent subsidiary to qualify as primary dealer.

NOTES

1. See the paper by Andrea Beltratti (1999) on the subject of asset allocation and EMU.
2. Council regulation 974/98 of 3 May 1998 on the introduction of the euro (*Official Journal* L 139 of 11.05.98).

3. See Fitch–IBCA, *Sovereign Comment, The Rating Impact of the Euro*, June 1998, and more recent statements by the firm.
4. As argued by William White of the BIS at the first meeting of the CEPS Working Party, 2 July 1997.
5. *Debt Redenomination and Market Convention in Stage III of EMU*, ad hoc Working Party of the Monetary Committee, European Commission, Euro Papers, No. 28, July 1998.
6. France and the Netherlands rounded to whole euros.
7. The actual/actual method, the most logical method, was prior to EMU fully applicable in only one country, France, the reason being that it made it complicated to calculate yields with a calculator, which explains the wide use of the other methods, such as 30/360. In the age of computers, however, this is no longer a problem.
8. For an overview of the conventions applicable and the implications of different day count conventions, see, *Debt Redenomination and Market Conventions in Stage 3 of EMU*, European Commission (1998) and the updates of this report; and Bank of England (1998).
9. Through a mortgage bond, a holder has a direct claim on the underlying real estate, which is not the case for mortgage-backed securities.

4
Governance and Policy

The overriding issues for policy-makers as a result of EMU reside in the alignment of the micro-controls in the functioning of capital markets and the macro-controls of financial markets in general. They are discussed in the last two sections of this chapter. Related are broader topics that are increasingly emerging as inconsistent with a single capital market: considerable differences in taxation of savings income and accounting standards, and rights attached to equity participations.

INCONSISTENCIES WITHIN A
SINGLE CAPITAL MARKET

Different national practices in taxation, accounting and corporate governance will increasingly prove to be incompatible with a single capital market. Whereas further harmonisation is required in taxation and accounting standards, market pressures and self-regulation can be expected to bring about more convergence in corporate governance.

Differences in Taxation and Related Regulations

The General Framework

The main reason why EMU does not immediately create a unified capital market is that investors and borrowers are subject to complicated fiscal regimes that differ greatly from one country to another, and these inconsistencies do not change immediately with the introduction of the euro. The importance of these variations is difficult to document systematically since there is no rule without an exception, and almost every country and every instrument is a special case. A few examples will suffice, however, to illustrate the significance of these differences in tax regimes for investors:

- In Germany, as in other EU member states, a withholding tax is levied on dividends, on which the company has already paid a 36% corporate tax. German residents can, however, receive a tax credit for the corporate income tax. This tax credit is not available to non-residents, but non-residents can, depending on the existence of a bilateral tax treaty, benefit from a lower withholding tax rate. Moreover, the German Ministry of Finance accords a tax credit only to dividends from firms based in Germany.
- In the UK, a system exists whereby a tax credit equivalent to the advance corporation tax paid by a local corporation is available for dividend income of UK residents. Some of the UK's double taxation treaties extend this tax credit to non-resident individuals and to institutional investors, but minus a 15% withholding tax. This tax credit is not applicable to foreign income dividends.
- In Italy, a dividend credit of 56.25% of the amount of the dividend applies to residents and local firms. This tax credit is only extended to France and the UK under double taxation treaties. Italy furthermore applies different withholding tax rates on interest income depending on the instrument. Income from Italian treasury bills is effectively taxed at a lower rate than bonds of other member states.[1]

Moreover, some European countries apply very low effective tax rates under certain circumstances which distort capital flows, such as the Irish Financial Services Centres or Belgium's Coordination Centres.

These are only a few examples from the tax jungle in Europe. It is hardly surprising if the international investor has some difficulty in discerning a forest from this confused jumble of trees. The basic issues are actually simple. Personal income taxation in all member countries is based on the world-wide principle: each individual (or household) is subject to the regime of the country of residence and should pay taxes there on the aggregated income from all sources. The problem is to ensure the application of this principle when there are large differences in the national tax regimes and when national tax administrations do not collaborate or exchange adequate information. Until now this has not been a major problem for most of the population because most income is earned from work (which is less mobile internationally) and the home bias of investors has ensured that—apart from corporations—only very rich individuals derived a significant fraction of their overall capital income from foreign sources. But this could change with the euro.

Two major issues posed by EMU are thus enforcement and compatibility. Enforcement is the first step. One has to ensure that 'foreign' income is actually declared before one can decide whether national tax regimes are compatible. Enforcement is therefore also the main concern at the EU level at present, and hence the current discussions on an EU-wide withholding tax on interest income.

As a result of EMU, discussions on the effective enforcement of taxation on income earned from capital have been placed back on the policy agenda. The agreement on taxation policy reached by the Council of EU Finance Ministers (Ecofin) on 1 December 1997 can be considered a major milestone in direct EU tax harmonisation. The Council agreed on a package of measures to combat *harmful* tax competition in the EU, including a code of conduct on corporate taxation and elements that should enable the Commission to draft a new proposal for a directive on the taxation of income from savings.[2] The Council invited the Tax Policy Group (or Monti Group) to continue its work and instituted a specific group to assess harmful tax competition. The first and at the same time the last EU measures so far in the area of direct taxation date back to 1990 and concern the abolition of double taxation on certain transactions between enterprises of the same group, and a common system of taxation for mergers.

The initiative to relaunch the EU tax policy debate was taken by Commissioner Monti at the informal Ecofin Council in Verona in April 1996. The Commissioner started from the overall assessment that taxation on income from work was becoming too heavy as a result of a downward spiral of unfair tax competition between the member states to attract investment. This was considered harmful since it led to a loss of tax revenue, distorted the single market and undermined employment. The Council agreed to the creation of an ad hoc group of special representatives of Finance Ministers under the chairmanship of Commissioner Monti, known as the Taxation Policy Group, whose deliberations resulted in the Ecofin agreement of 1 December 1997.

A central element of the package is the Code of Conduct by which member states agree not to introduce new tax measures that are harmful and to eliminate existing harmful tax measures, the so-called 'standstill' and 'rollback' procedures. According to the Council, harmful tax measures are those providing for a significantly lower effective level of taxation, including zero taxation, than that which generally applies in the member states and in the Community as a whole.

To ensure that this does not become a dead letter, the Council agreed to the creation of a forum for regular consultation between the member states to discuss and comment on any new tax measure that might fall within the scope of the code. This 'Code of Conduct Group' will report regularly to the Ecofin Council. A first interim report was presented to the 1 December 1998 Ecofin Council, listing some 85 potentially harmful tax measures.

Although corporate taxation does not directly fall within the scope of this paper, it is clearly linked with taxation of interest and dividend income. In some member states, for example, a tax credit for dividend income can be obtained for corporate taxes paid by a firm. Luxembourg requested that a future directive on withholding taxes should be accompanied by a directive on corporate taxation, as was mentioned in the 1 December 1997 Ecofin Conclusions.

The basic principle of the draft directive on interest income, which was presented by the European Commission on 20 May 1998, is that an EU citizen from any member state should no longer be considered a 'foreigner' by tax administrations in another member state, while earning interest income in that state. Until now tax administrations did not care whether non-residents declared their income or not in their home country because the loss of revenue was a problem for a foreign country. Under the new directive, a 20% withholding tax would be applied to interest accrued in whatever form (also capitalisation of interest income) on all kinds of debt securities (including the former Euro-bonds, and UCITS which invest more than 50% of their assets in debt-claims), and paid in one member state to individuals who are resident in another member state, but it would not apply to non-EU citizens. The collection of the withholding tax would be carried out by the paying agent.[3]

Although tight deadlines have been set by the Council, reaching an agreement on the draft directive on the taxation of savings (which is only the first element in the overall work programme) still promises to be a Herculean task. Witness the heated discussions in some member states on the necessity of the proposal, and the fear for capital outflows. The 1 December 1997 Ecofin Conclusions could in this respect be recalled. The French delegation, for example, requested a minimum withholding tax rate of 25%, whereas the UK stated that the directive should not apply to Euro-bonds and similar instruments (without specifying what the meaning of Euro-bonds would be under EMU, see Box 4.1). These discussions remind one of the fate of the 1989 draft directive on the harmonisation of withholding taxes, which had to be withdrawn by the European Commission.[4]

One practical problem with the planned European withholding tax (which would be EU-wide, not just EMU-wide) is that two systems of capital income taxation are applied in the EU, one where withholding taxes are levied directly when interest income is received, and the other where this income is reported to the tax authorities and added to the income tax declaration (a reporting system—RS). Although the latter is applied only by two small countries, both systems would co-exist under the Council Conclusions, whereby either a withholding tax would be applied or information on savings income obtained in host member states would be provided to tax authorities in the home member state.

An overview of general (resident) withholding tax rates and the tax system applicable in EU member states is given in Table 4.1. This is an assessment of the official rule, to which many

Table 4.1 *Resident withholding taxes on interest and dividends in the EU (1997)*

	Withholding Tax		Application
	Interest Income	Dividends	
B	15	25	Final
DK	RS	25	(RS)
DE	25	25	Not final
EL	15	0	Final
E	25	25	Not final
F	25	25	Final
I	12.5	12.5	Final
IRL	24	0	Final
L	0	25	Not final
NL	RS	25	(RS)
AU	25	25	Final
P	20	30	Final
SF	28	28	Final
SW	30	30	Not final
UK	20	0	Not final
CH	35	35	Not final
US	RS	30	(RS)

Source: Price Waterhouse (1997).

variations and exceptions exist. In most EU states, withholding taxes are in principle also levied on non-residents, except in Austria, Luxembourg and Sweden, or when a reporting system applies. De facto, however, non-residents pay no withholding taxes in most EU countries, since the tax is not applied by the paying agent and the rules are not enforced. Also under the reporting system, non-residents benefit, since there is still little exchange of information between tax administrations.

In theory, withholding taxes are only a means to ensure that income is actually declared so that it can be effectively taxed. Withholding taxes are often final on cross-border investments, however, since national tax administrations give only partial credit to taxes withheld abroad, and procedures for tax credits on taxes withheld at source often discriminate against non-residents, or do not apply to them, as illustrated above. Moreover, some national tax administrations are known to take years to actually pay reimbursements for excess taxes. Thus, even a uniform European-wide withholding tax could be perceived differently from one country to another.

A detailed review of the tax regimes applicable in EU member states would exceed the scope of this paper. These examples are only intended to give a flavour of the mixture of the different kinds of treatment that are applied within the EU today based on the 'nationality' of the instrument and of the investor, which might keep markets fragmented for some time to come.

It should be emphasised that the focus of the analysis here is not on the general level of taxation, but on the distribution of the burden between different factors of production and market segments. It can certainly be argued that the current overall level of taxation in Europe is too high, especially in those countries where the governments take close to one-half of GDP. Our point is that it is not economically efficient to have a structure in which tax rates vary enormously. Recent research shows that the high tax rates on labour have been responsible for high unemployment and lower growth (Daveri and Tabellini 1997). A mixture of heavy taxation of labour with zero taxation of capital is economically inappropriate. This is not just a question of perceived fairness, but a recognition that governments have a responsibility to ensure that income from capital is taxed at an appropriate level. What constitutes an appropriate level, of course, is the subject of serious debate. We would argue that it should fall at the lower end of the range, but this is not the purpose of this chapter.

Matters Related to Euro-bonds

The favourable tax treatment of Euro-bonds (i.e. Xeno-bonds) deserves particular emphasis. The current definition of Euro-bonds (see Box 4.1) does not make sense in a common currency area. If markets became really integrated, all public and private issues could be sold throughout the EMU area and financial institutions from several countries would routinely assist in their placement. This would imply that if one did not change the definition of 'Euro-bonds', practically all new issues of public and private bonds would qualify as 'Euro', and hence be tax exempt.

The lighter regime for Euro securities was based on the assumption that only institutions and wealthy households would dare to invest across borders. With institutional investors, there is in general no problem with tax evasion and in the case of wealthy individuals, they are difficult to tax owing to their highly mobile lifestyle. Under EMU, even small retail investors will routinely buy paper issued in euros by 'foreign' governments in the area, and issued by institutions that are foreign, but within the EMU area. Many of these securities are currently classified as having the status of 'Euro-bonds', but they should be treated as domestic bonds. In this sense, the status of 'Euro-bonds' should be extended only to issues that come from outside the EU or, at least, outside the EMU area. If this were done, it is likely that more than a third of all the issues that are currently classified as Euro-bonds would become ordinary domestic issues.

Box 4.1   From Euro- to Xeno-bonds

One of the hallmarks of Euro-bonds is their exemption from withholding tax. Most Euro-bonds carry a commitment by the issuer that if a withholding tax is subsequently applied to interest payments, either the bond will be redeemed or the interest payment augmented by the size of the tax (Benzie 1992). The UK argued that this exemption from withholding taxes should be enshrined in a future EU directive. In the meantime, however, it is clear that the commonly applied definition of what constitutes a 'Euro-bond' will have to change with the introduction of the euro. The name has clearly become a source of confusion and could better be 'Xeno-bonds'.

The existing definition in European law of what constitutes a Euro-security would not formally be affected by EMU since, somewhat surprisingly, it has nothing to do with the currency of issue. The 1989 prospectus directive, discussed in more detail below, specifies:

(f) 'Euro-securities' shall mean transferable securities which:

- are to be underwritten and distributed by a syndicate at least two of the members of which have their registered offices in different States, and
- are offered on a significant scale in one or more States other than that of the issuer's registered office, and
- may be subscribed for or initially acquired only through a credit institution or other financial institution.

On the basis of this and other financial market definitions, it would essentially mean that many bonds issued in the euro zone would qualify as Euro-bonds, and would therefore be exempt from taxes! This situation will have to be changed, or there will no longer be any grounds on which to enforce taxes on interest income. This problem, however, will not be an easy one to tackle as long as some EU countries stay outside EMU, including the country that currently arranges most Euro-bond issues.

EU Withholding Taxes and Financial Centres

Two facts are routinely ignored in the discussions concerning the issue of applying the proposed new EU-wide withholding tax on interest income to Euro-bonds.

First the key fact: the proposed directive would apply to all interest payments to individuals; it would therefore not discriminate between the issuer or the form of the bond. There is consequently absolutely no reason why the issuance of Euro-bonds should be affected by it. Euro-bonds issued from a tax haven would not be more attractive to investors based in the EU. The fears that EU financial centres would suffer as the Euro-bond business shifts abroad because of the EU withholding tax are unfounded. Those wishing to hide their interest income might want to hold their assets in places that ensure anonymity, but this is independent of what type of bond they hold. Providing a safe haven for tax evaders has anyway never been an important business for places such as London, although it may be more the case for Luxembourg.

The second fact: the proposed withholding tax is not a new, additional tax, but merely a device to ensure that existing national taxes on interest income can actually be enforced. Apart from a small loss in terms of the timing of cash flows, a withholding tax does not affect honest tax payers. This consideration has implications for the grandfathering issue. Most Euro-bond issues contain a clause that allows the issuer to recall the bonds at par if a withholding tax is imposed. Originally introduced to protect investors, this clause would now benefit the borrowers because interest rates are now much lower than when most Euro-bonds were issued. It is often argued that such an ex-post transfer is undesirable and should be avoided by exempting (grandfathering) outstanding Euro-bond issues under the EU directive. From an economic point of view this argument is not tenable. Unanticipated income transfers have to a first approximation no overall welfare implications, they are just a zero sum game within the private sector. Moreover, governments would gain some additional revenue to the extent that tax payers were previously not honest. As the bonds already exist, this would amount to a lump sum tax—the most efficient form of raising revenue for economists. Moreover, one cannot really argue that the withholding tax could not be anticipated; the very existence of the clause allowing redemption in this case shows this.

Therefore there are no economic arguments for an extensive grandfathering of existing Euro-bonds. It is up to borrowers to decide whether they want to use a clause inserted to protect investors for their own benefit and thus lose the trust of savers.

Given the facts, what are the practical issues?

Before EMU Euro-bonds were in most places a foreign currency bond. The implicit justification for subjecting Euro-bonds to a lighter regulatory and fiscal regime was that small savers generally did not invest in foreign currency bonds whereas institutional investors can watch out for themselves and are generally transparent for the fiscal authorities, so that there was no need for measures to ensure an effective taxation of this type of bond. But the principle that country = currency is no longer valid within the euro zone. Bonds issued anywhere in the euro zone will be considered as domestic bonds even by small savers. A bond issued in euros by Electricité de France and placed by a syndicate consisting of German, French and other participants will appeal to small investors throughout Euroland. There is no reason to give it special fiscal treatment. Note that the US tax authorities are very stringent in enforcing the effective taxation of interest income and make no exemptions for Euro-bonds.

The key issue that remains for London and other financial centres in the EU is thus only whether one should continue to apply the lighter regulatory regime to Xeno-bonds in terms of prospectus requirements, and so on. If this were changed there would indeed be a reason to de-localise the issuance of such bonds to financial centres with a lighter regulatory burden. The US does not seem to be a particularly attractive alternative since the US Securities and Exchange Commission (SEC) is known to be much more intrusive than its European counterparts, but other competitors might arise. This is a legitimate issue that the national authorities responsible for financial centres should pursue, namely to ensure that the regulatory framework for the nascent European capital market is not so heavy that it drives legitimate business off-shore.

The withholding tax issue illustrates a strategic problem the UK will have to face as long as it remains outside EMU. Tax codes are based on the principle 'country = currency' which is no longer valid within the euro zone, and its governments will increasingly have to coordinate their tax policy on a wide range of issues. The UK must decide whether it wants to cooperate pragmatically or impede the other member states in addressing a serious practical problem. A systematic use of the veto on tax issues would only force the euro-zone countries to put the issue of qualified majority voting on tax issues on the agenda for the next intergovernmental conference, thereby establishing the variable geometry the UK has so far successfully resisted. Opposition on principle to the withholding tax proposals does not safeguard any British interests but could do lasting political damage.

Accounting Standards

The lack of confidence in the financial information published in other member states is an important reason for the limited integration of Europe's securities markets. Harmonisation of accounting standards has not gone sufficiently far, and consequently mutual recognition does not work. A commonly accepted accounting standard would ease cross-border listing and offers of securities. Since offers of securities need to contain detailed disclosures on the issuers' financial situation and prospects, and the rights attached to the securities, local differences in valuing assets, liabilities, profits and losses heavily influence cross-border acceptance of these securities. This problem becomes even more acute in EMU, but because of the international dimension of the debate, no solution is evident.

The EU has adopted several directives regarding harmonisation of basic accounting standards, auditing of accounts and rules on disclosure. The most important are the fourth, seventh and eighth company law directives, which deal with the annual accounts, the consolidation principles and the auditors' qualifications of limited liability companies. The accounting directives, however, accommodate the basic practices in place at the moment but do not yet impose European accounting standards, as too many implementation options are left to the member states: 62 in the fourth directive, 50 in the seventh. Moreover, great differences exist between EU states with respect to the interpretation of these provisions and the enforcement process leaves much to be desired. Mutual recognition of accounts published in another member state is not working. Further harmonisation of accounting standards aimed at reaching a European standard has, until recently, therefore been the priority.

Different conceptual frameworks exist in EU member states, which explains the persistent differences in accounting practices (FEE 1997). They can, generally speaking, be reduced to two broad national traditions in accounting: one in which the process is driven by the needs of financial markets and the other in which it is primarily driven by law—the former represented mainly by the English-speaking countries (and to a certain extent by the Netherlands) and the latter by the other continental Western European countries. In the former grouping, the accounts are expected to convey information of an adequate quality, in accordance with the currently accepted standards and practices developed by the profession. In the latter, it is based on compliance with statutory requirements. The tax authorities have retained a strong influence on the accounting regulation processes in these countries, as national laws state that the taxable profit should be very close to the profit reported in the individual financial statements. Setting an overall conceptual framework for accounting could deprive these authorities of their influence.

The listing of Daimler–Benz on the New York Stock Exchange (1994) gave an important stimulus to the discussions on harmonisation of accounting practices. It showed that the globalisation of capital markets was driving the debate and that the dominant market was setting the tune. To comply with the listing rules, Daimler–Benz had to adopt US GAAP (Generally Accepted Accounting Principles), which led to totally different financial results than were produced under German accounting rules, for which the firm had to pay a premium. Other German corporations, such as Deutsche Telecom, Hoechst and VEBA, have followed suit in the meantime.

The dual accounts situation is confusing, however, for shareholders and financial analysts. The question arises as to which standard should be used to assess the performance and prospects of a firm. Contrary to what might be thought at first, double accounting does not necessarily allow for better decisions because it provides more information. Rather, it tends to create an information overload and a credibility problem. On the other hand, it makes life easier for the investment community. Analysts and fund managers base their valuations of accounts on the accounting language they are the most familiar with. As a result of the dominance of US capital markets, US GAAP is also the best known accounting language. In instances where accounts are published in only one accounting language, analysts will not bother to make the calculations of how the accounts would look in the other. Accounts might thus look more or less attractive to a potential investor if they were published in the accounting language with which he is familiar, but since this work is so complicated, the job is not undertaken, and the stock consequently is not bought or sold. Hence, international portfolio diversification is constrained and willingness to invest abroad is significantly reduced.[5]

In the light of this development, the policy choice, as seen from a European perspective, became much clearer: either the dominance of US GAAP is accepted, and governments outside the US accept accounting principles over which they have no influence, or agreement is reached on one set of international accounting standards (IAS) within the International Accounting Standards Committee (IASC). For the European Commission, the choice was obvious: the agreement between IASC and the international organisation of securities supervisors (IOSCO), to agree on one set of IAS to be accepted by all stock exchanges as part of the listing requirements, should be supported. In this context, insistence on further European harmonisation of accounts is superfluous, as it leads to double accounting and, in the long run, would lend more weight to the US GAAP.[6]

Acceptance of this evolution requires the compliance of national and European accounting practices with IAS. It also requires that a flexible method be devised that allows for changes to be introduced in the European directives for changes in IAS, without being accompanied each time by formal amendments. EU accounting directives as they stand today do not allow companies to comply with IAS. The European Commission is therefore examining the possibility of amending the fourth directive as well as creating a flexible mechanism for future adaptations. Developments at the member state level, however, are not so clear. Some member states, such as Belgium and Germany, have accepted reports prepared solely on the basis of US GAAP, or a combination of US GAAP alongside the national accounting system, which has the effect of undermining greater political support for IAS. Other member states, such as France, have gone in the other direction and accepted IAS. It should be clear that member states cannot exempt firms from complying with EU law, however, which means that it is illegal for European firms to use US GAAP exclusively, but also that amendments to the existing directives to make them comply with IAS are urgently needed.

At international level, uncertainty over the acceptance of IAS by the most powerful member of IOSCO, the US Securities and Exchange Commission, is widespread, and may take years to be settled. The Chairman of the SEC, Arthur Levitt, recently criticised US accounting standards for being insufficiently refined, which spells little good for IAS. On the other hand, US GAAP is spreading further in Europe, with the DaimlerChrysler group applying US GAAP as the single standard for the whole group, as well as for internal reporting purposes. In an effort to give maximum credit to IAS, the European Commission has, in the context of the Financial Services Policy Group, signalled (January 1999) that IAS should be mandatory for all listed companies. Furthermore, it has requested the European Securities Commissions to screen the standards developed by the IASC in their conformity with EU rules. But it seems that it is already too late.

The Wider Corporate Governance Framework

Discontent with the quality of financial reporting and control is one of the driving forces behind the corporate governance debates in Europe. It was the direct motive for the establishment of the Cadbury Committee in the UK in 1991, and it has also been the subject of discussion in other prominent committees which have published their findings in the meantime, most importantly the Viénot (France) and Peters (the Netherlands) reports. It is interesting to note that all three committees stressed that this area should not be subject to statutory legislation, but that improvements should be realised through self-regulation by the corporate sector and peer pressure. Companies have to indicate in their annual reports to what extent they comply with a local Code and explain any instances of non-compliance. However, a European dimension is absent from the domestic debates, which probably explains the stalemate on EU harmonisation measures in the area of company law.[7]

That the corporate governance debate first emerged in the UK among the European countries should not be surprising. Its equity market is the most developed in the EU, consisting of many quoted companies and highly dispersed shareholdings, which are mostly in the hands of institutional investors. The UK debate was triggered by cases of bad corporate control, and high levels of executive pay in privatised corporations. It spilled over to continental Europe and, even though the circumstances are different, committees have been established in several European countries. In France and the Netherlands, recommendations have been published, while reports are being finalised in Belgium, Italy and Spain.

Overall, some common principles can be extracted from these discussions regarding auditing and reporting, the role of boards, and the preferred method for moving ahead. In order to improve the quality of reporting and to preserve shareholders' equity, all three corporate governance committees stressed the need to appoint audit committees within companies, requested boards to state that internal control procedures were going on and to maintain clear relationships with company auditors, which should be sufficiently independent. To guarantee the quality of control, companies need strong boards, composed of well-qualified executive directors and truly independent non-executives. It has been suggested that the position of chairman and CEO is best split, and that the number of board mandates per person should be limited. As for the means for making further progress, there is also a clear agreement between all the committees: self-regulation is preferable to statutory changes in existing legislation.

The results of the corporate governance committees also contain disappointing elements. There is a willingness to change board procedures in continental Europe, but not to alter the relationship between companies and shareholders or the structure of the annual general meeting (AGM). The Viénot and Peters Committees do not propose to amend limitations on shareholder rights or to encourage shareholder participation in AGMs. The question thereby arises whether the local corporate governance committees, at least in continental Europe, really want change. The Cadbury and above all the new Hampel reports, on the other hand, require institutional shareholders to vote at AGMs and to take their share of responsibility as investors. Also, the European dimension of the debate was not raised by any of the committees. However, globalisation, of which the European Single Market is an element, is mentioned as a reason for reforming the national corporate control system steps at national borders.

The preference for self-regulation and the absence of a European dimension in the national corporate governance committees are not making the ongoing efforts in company law harmonisation any easier at European level. Key harmonisation proposals concerning the legal structure of corporations, takeover bid procedures and the European Company Statute have been blocked before the EU Council of Ministers for many years, and it will be difficult to make progress. The reason for the deadlock is often reduced to the issue of worker participation in corporate control: workers' representatives are entitled to have seats on the boards of corporations in Denmark, Germany and the Netherlands, and a lighter structure at European level could bring these national systems under pressure.

Other sensitive issues, however, also hamper the harmonisation of corporate governance structures in the EU, such as the
powers and responsibilities of shareholders and boards, the
existence of barriers to takeovers, the discretionary powers of
governments, and taxation. It finally comes back to the question of whether further statutory harmonisation is desirable and
necessary in an area where change is already very difficult to
implement even at national levels.

Take for example the issue of control rights. Draft EU
company law directives incorporated language providing for
equal treatment of shareholders and the 'one share-one vote'
principle. It is clear that this is not the general rule among EU
member states. Voting rights can also be double or multiple;
they can be limited under a certain ceiling (capped); or shares
might have no voting rights at all. Table 4.2 gives a general
overview of voting rights in the EU and, for purposes of
comparison, Switzerland and the US. This is an assessment of
the most common situation, which is not only a matter of
company law, but also of practice within companies. In the UK,
for example, exceptions to the 'one share-one vote' principle
are allowed by law, but they have become rare, because of the
preference of institutional investors for a simple structure.

Double or multiple voting rights are common in all
Scandinavian countries, in France and in the Netherlands. In
France, double voting rights can be authorised as part of the
clauses in the articles of incorporation or in the bylaws, under
certain conditions. They cease automatically in the event of a
share transfer, which makes them a form of anti-takeover
device. French management is said to be strongly in favour of
keeping this option.[8] Multiple voting rights in Finland can be
granted for a maximum of 20 votes per share; in Sweden, they
must not exceed ten times the right of ordinary shares. The
circulation of double or multiple voting shares allows high
liquidity of stocks with large ownership blocks, but they could
depress prices for ordinary shares if investors view these as
having inferior voting value. Non-voting shares exist in most
EU countries, where such securities may get a higher dividend
in return for fewer ownership rights but they are generally
limited up to a certain percentage. They are not allowed in

Table 4.2   *Dominant form of shares and voting rights in the EU*

Shares	Dominant form	Multiple voting rights	Non-voting shares	Capped voting
A	Bearer	No	Yes	Yes
B	Bearer	No	Yes	Dep. on bylaws (< 20%)
D	Bearer	No	Yes	Dep. on bylaws
DK	Registered	Yes (<10x)	No	Yes
E	bearer	No	Yes	Yes
F	Bearer	Yes (<2x)	Yes	Yes
FIN	Registered	Yes (<20x)	No	Yes
GR	Registered	No	Yes	No
IRL	Registered	No	No	No
I	Registered	No	Yes (< 50%)	Yes
L	Bearer	No	Yes	No
NL	Bearer	Yes	Yes	Yes, see bylaws
P	Bearer	No	Yes	No
SW	Registered	Yes (<10x)	No	Yes (< 20%)
UK	Registered	Uncommon	Uncommon	Uncommon
CH	Registered	Yes	Yes	Yes, see bylaws
US	Registered	Uncommon	Uncommon	No

Sources: European Commission (1995b), Davis and Lannoo (1998).

Denmark, Ireland and Sweden. Harmonising EU legislation in the area of control rights could thus eliminate some forms of barriers to takeovers that exist in EU member states. This would be opposed by employers, or even governments, which would prefer to keep the 'national champions' free from takeover threats.

With a view to finding a compromise in the EU Council, these sensitive issues have been dropped from the latest draft under discussion of the *regulation* of the European Company Statute, the optional legal structure for companies operating with a single incorporation in the EU. Compared to the first draft, proposed in the early 1970s, the regulation has become more of a framework measure, from which many sensitive issues have been omitted and referred to national law. It concerns not only tax issues, but also the protection of creditors, the liability of directors, the voting rules in the general assembly, and so forth. The regulation, which is in EU law a legal instrument that is directly applicable in the member states, has in practice become more of a *directive*, which is to be implemented in national legislation. As with other difficult directives, this approach can be expected to hamper cross-border recognition.

The European Commission has recently hardened its line on shareholder restrictions in privatised companies. So far, member states' desire to keep privatised corporations nationally 'anchored', has not met with objections from the European Commission, although it went against the Treaty principle on free capital movement. In several European member states, privatisations were placed with local companies and investors, or governments tried to maintain control through specific legal constructions. Recently, however, the European Commission has threatened to bring member states before the European Court on unequal shareholder rights in privatised companies in Belgium, France, Italy, Portugal and Spain.[9]

The growing strength and importance of institutional investors in continental Europe and the increasing importance of equity capital in their portfolios will further stimulate the debate on adequate corporate governance. As discussed above, EMU changes the asset allocation patterns of European institutional investors, diminishing the home bias in investments and increasing the share of equity investments. Since investors will be in open competition in asset mix and portfolio returns, a deeper and more active posture with respect to their equity investments can be expected, following the example of US institutional investors.

Integration of capital markets as a result of EMU will underline the European dimension of the debate. The strong similarity in the conclusions of the national semi-official corporate governance committees should lead European industry, if not the European Commission, to recommend a European-wide code of best practice.[10] Even at the global level, there is agreement on best practice in corporate governance, as shown by recent initiatives by the OECD in this area.[11] The need for a common standard within the EU, however, is much greater, because of the existence of a common legal framework, a single market and a single currency. Such a European Code should function as a minimum standard, and could easily point to the lacunae in local codes. It would also bring more convergence in the European corporate governance systems, and could serve as a benchmark for the Central and Eastern European countries in the approximation of laws process.

At a minimum, the European policy-makers could focus on a more modest policy agenda and simply work to harmonise practices which would better allow investors to work in Europe as one market. Notices for AGMs, procedures to vote at AGMs, voting by mail, and so on, differ from market to market, and keep national boundaries in place. These issues will need to be tackled soon, as investors will look on the euro zone as one market. These steps should, however, be seen as narrow, short-term measures only and not be allowed to dampen the impetus towards a European initiative in corporate governance.

THE IMPLICATIONS OF EMU FOR CAPITAL MARKET SUPERVISION

To organise the discussion of what EMU implies for capital markets, it is useful to distinguish between financial and prudential controls. Prudential rules operate at the macro-level to protect clients' money and to prevent systemic crises. They are of importance to financial markets in general and are usually laid down in legislation. Financial controls function at the micro-level, that is at the level of the firm. They must guarantee the integrity of markets, by ensuring the equal treatment of participants, transparency of operations and fairness of trades. Their regulation is more a part of conduct-of-business rules and is laid down in 'soft' rules by the different markets.

The questions that emerge with EMU differ for each case. In the case of financial market controls, the issue is the insufficient degree of harmonisation of rules and cooperation between supervisors. In the case of prudential supervision, harmonisation has largely been achieved at EU and international level;

rather the question emerges of the optimal institutional structure for prudential control, the need for more centralisation and
the structure of cooperation with the (European) central bank.
The former issues are raised in this section, whereas the latter
are discussed in the following section.

The EU Framework

Rules on capital markets concern issuers, intermediaries and
investors, and markets. The main EU harmonising directive
regarding capital markets is the investment services directive
(ISD): it sets the conditions for the single licence of investment
firms, the rules for access to and control of organised securities markets, and the protection of investors. Other rules
harmonise conditions for issuers of securities and operations in
capital markets.

The Regulation of Intermediaries and Markets in the ISD

At the time of the negotiations, the ISD gave rise to heated
debates between the member states. The directive had become
synonymous for 'red tape' and over-regulation. This has over-
shadowed the liberalising effects of the directive, the facility of
'remote membership', which allows investment firms to be a
member of an organised securities market across borders,
without being established in the country of that market, or
exchanges to put their screens with traders in other member
states. Moreover, hot issues in the ISD debate in the years
1991–1992, such as banks' access to stock exchanges or on- and
off-exchange trading, have become irrelevant in the meantime,
as a result of the market developments discussed in Chapter 2.

The ISD follows the principles of the other financial services
single licence directives: subject to complying with certain basic
business conditions, an investment firm is granted a single
licence to offer its services all over the EU, after due notification

of its plans in other member states to its home authorities, which are in charge of final supervision. The scope for host country control is, however, wider than in the banking directives. When providing services across borders or trading on a regulated market of another member state, an investment firm must observe the local conduct-of-business rules. Compliance has to be checked in the member state where the service is provided. These rules are very broadly defined in Article 11 of the ISD. It requires that firms act honestly, with due care and diligence, while making adequate disclosure, in the best interest of their clients and the integrity of the market. Firms need to try to avoid conflicts of interest in the different functions they exercise, and when they cannot be avoided, to ensure that their clients are fairly treated. Host country member states can ask foreign firms to provide information regarding compliance with the local rules (Art. 19). Investment firms need to report all trades in shares, bonds and futures instruments carried out on regulated markets to the competent authorities. The relevant files on all transactions must be kept for five years.

The directive should not give *carte blanche* for an unrestrained and protectionist application of host state rules to foreign providers of services. Rules of conduct must be applied 'in such a way as to take account of the professional nature of the person to whom the service is provided' (Art. 11.3), which allows for a distinction between retail and wholesale investors. Discriminatory rules are prohibited (Art. 28). Investment firms may, however, as a result, be subject to overlapping or conflicting rules of conduct, the rules of the home and the host country (Wouters 1997). Article 11 requires member states, without distinction, to draw up rules of conduct, which must be observed 'at all times'.

The second freedom the directive institutes is the freedom of an organised trading system, classified as a 'regulated market', to have remote access in another member state. The directive says that a member state must allow the regulated market of other member states to provide 'appropriate facilities' within its territories, to give investment firms the freedoms of the directive (Art 15.4). These facilities are screens by which an operator can have remote access to a stock exchange of another

EU country. According to the directive, a regulated market is a market that: (i) functions regularly; (ii) is governed by regulations on operation as approved by the authorities and on access, set out in the 1979 directive on the conditions for official stock exchange listing (79/279/EEC); and (iii) complies with rules on reporting and transparency of trades as set by the directive (Art. 1.13). The freedoms of the directive are thus only granted to markets which comply with these requirements. A first list of regulated markets was published in the EU's *Official Journal* (*OJ* C 203, 1997). Updates followed in December 1998 (COM(1998)780) and May 1999 (*OJ* C 151, 1999). It comprises all securities and derivatives markets of the EU. Some countries have also included their primary dealer markets.

Even if the harmonisation of structure of securities markets was not part of the original Commission draft (1989), the concept of a regulated market emerged during the Council discussions. Regulated markets were contrasted to over-the-counter transactions (OTC), whereby the former were characterised by the principles of transparency, fairness and security, the latter by the opposite thereof, fragmentation and reduced liquidity. On the basis of a logical analysis, this distinction is rather problematic, but it was included for protectionist motives, that is to counter the dominance of London's SEAQ International at that time. It would have allowed member states to forbid their firms to transact domestic shares through the London Stock Exchange. The text thus incorporates provisions to mandate that transactions are carried out on a regulated market (the 'concentration' provision, Art. 14.3) and to ensure transparency through regular publication of prices and volumes (Art. 21). In order to obtain final approval of the text, exceptions were incorporated to allow for off-regulated market transactions and for non-application of the transparency requirements for large blocks of shares.[12]

The difficulty of defining market structures for exchanges is not typically European, but a global problem for securities regulators. A close definition of an exchange seems to be very complex. Exchanges around the globe differ profoundly in their role, functions, and governance structures, and these elements are in rapid evolution as a result of technology and competition.

The range of functions an exchange performs connected to the execution of trades differs across countries. Human trade disintermediation is under pressure everywhere from electronic auction systems. Exchanges struggle with member representation systems, and are being transformed from cooperative and non-profit structures into for-profit organisations. This last point raises the question about the obligatory dissemination of price information data. Could exchanges that have become private entities be forced to publicly and regularly publish information on prices and quotes, as the ISD requires?

On the whole, views on the regulation of securities markets depend on the priorities in the objectives to be obtained. Proponents of price and quote transparency, the most influential supporter of which has been the US Securities and Exchange Commission, believe that it promotes all the goals securities regulation should deliver, namely: investor protection, fairness, competition, market efficiency, liquidity, market integrity and investor confidence. But according to Lee (1998: pp. 270–271), price transparency primarily serves the goal of investor protection, particularly of retail investors, and can compromise efficiency and liquidity. The UK regulatory authorities, for example, have concentrated more on efficiency, the primary concern for institutional investors. For Lee, price and quote transparency should be viewed as a mechanism, not as a regulatory objective per se.

The ISD thus covers the regulation and supervision of intermediaries and the markets in which these firms are active, but only the regulated markets. This is not necessarily carried out by the same authority or in the same way in the different member states. In France, for example, different bodies are responsible for the supervision of the markets and intermediaries.[13] Such a situation does not facilitate cooperation and exchange of information, which is of even greater importance in EMU. Member states first need to ensure cooperation between the different authorities on their own territory, which is already a difficult task. There is often a tension between internal and self-regulatory supervision by the market and the statutory supervision of the market. Secondly, cooperation between these different authorities needs to be ensured at EU level.

Listing Admission and Disclosure

Already, back in 1979, the Community had adopted harmonised requirements for admission of securities to official stock exchange listing. The directive specifies the conditions for admission of equity and debt securities, and the obligations for issuers. To qualify for stock exchange listing, a minimum of 25% of the subscribed capital of a firm should be distributed to the public. When shares are admitted, companies need to ensure equal treatment of shareholders, enable them to exercise their rights and make all necessary information available. Shareholders need to be informed of meetings and enabled to exercise their right to vote. Major new developments which may lead to substantial movements in share prices, changes in share rights and the shareholding structure need to be made public as soon as possible.

Disclosure of major holdings was made the subject of a separate directive ten years later. The directive covering the publication of information on major holdings (1988) sets minimum rules for the disclosure of information when a major shareholding in a company listed on an EC stock exchange is acquired or disposed of. Information has to be made public when the proportion of voting rights held reaches, exceeds or falls below the thresholds of 10, 20, 33, 50 and 76%. It took several member states considerably more time than anticipated to implement and enforce the directive. Major German banks and insurance companies, for example, only started to reveal their holdings in 1996. A recent study on ownership concentration in Europe (Becht 1997) found that the practical implementation of the major holdings directive is not satisfactory and that the directive is failing to achieve its objective. Since shareholding is concentrated in continental Europe, it is of the utmost importance that small investors are informed of changes in large blockholdings in order to sustain their confidence in equity markets. The study calls for more mandatory disclosure rules at the European level, since self-regulation cannot ensure their quality and effectiveness.

Mutual Recognition of Listing Particulars

Once securities are listed on one EU stock exchange, securities particulars and public offer prospectuses are to be granted mutual recognition throughout the EU. Minimal harmonisation and mutual recognition of securities particulars are basically governed by two directives: (i) the listing particulars directive, covering the listing particulars of securities in an organised market in the EU; and (ii) the prospectus directive, regarding initial public offerings of securities in EU capital markets in general. The former directive dates back to 1980, but was amended in 1987 to achieve mutual recognition of listing particulars, and again in 1990 to achieve mutual recognition of public-offer prospectuses as listing particulars.[14] In theory, one member state's approval for listing is extended mutual recognition by the others. Home country disclosure requirements, which are at least as strict as the minimum required by the directive, are to be recognised mutually. The 1989 prospectus directive covers all securities in general, including unit trusts, debt and equity securities, and Euro-securities.[15] It defines the required content of securities prospectuses when they are offered to the public. This must contain information to enable the investor 'to make an informed assessment of the assets and liabilities, financial position, profit and losses and prospects of the issuer and of the rights attaching to the transferable securities' (Art. 11). Once a prospectus has been approved in one member state, it receives mutual recognition in the others.

The problem with the listing particulars directive is that it failed to remove many impediments to a greater integration of securities markets and left open opportunities for host country control. The minimum disclosure standard of the directive is often too low for mutual recognition to work. It would mean that the listing particulars of less developed capital markets of the EU would have to be accepted in the more developed ones. De facto, the directives were not sufficiently comprehensive. Listing particulars need to be published in the language of the host country, they need to carry information on the income tax system, and they cease to be valid after three months. The prospectus directive allows for a 12-month validity. The utility of the directive, however, is undermined by the fact that Euro-securities have been interpreted by most member states as being bonds. Furthermore, advertising rules can be restricted by the host country. More fundamentally, mutual recognition of the prospectus is sometimes simply not provided for in national law. As a consequence, the offering of securities on a pan-European basis is hampered. According to Stanislas Yassukovich, Chairman of EASDAQ, the stock exchange for high-growth European stocks, European securities issuers are caught in a maze of legal technicalities which inhibit potential high-growth ventures. He actually sees fewer problems for equities of non-European issuers which are distributed more freely in Europe than for shares of European companies.[16]

Tackling Insider Dealing

The insider dealing directive of 1989 coordinated the rules governing treatment of this activity and made it a statutory offence. Previously, several member states placed no statutory restraint against insider dealing, and the regulations that did exist differed widely. As with the major holdings directive, implementation did not come about smoothly. Germany, for example, only implemented the directive in 1995, four years after the required date. Even today, several EU member states are still unsure of how best to deal with the phenomenon of insider dealing, and enforcement differs widely, according to a recent Commission study on implementation. In some member states, such as the UK and France, where a law on this subject existed before the Community directive was enacted, many legal trials of insider trading have been reported. In other countries, such as the Netherlands, Belgium, Denmark or Germany, there have only been very few instances. Cooperation between authorities is said to be working, however, and insider trading is explicitly part of the memoranda of understanding between supervisors.

Securities Market Regulation in EMU and Beyond

Increased development and integration of securities markets, which will result from EMU, requires policy-makers' action on three fronts: further harmonisation of conduct-of-business rules in the ISD, a level playing field for cross-border listing and initial public offerings of securities; and increased cooperation among supervisors. Technological developments and the spread of the Internet will require action to harmonise basic requirements for firms managing trading systems.

Further harmonisation in conduct-of-business rules in the ISD is required to ease cross-border provision of services. This would allow firms to provide services across borders under home country conduct-of-business rules, rather than under the host rules, as is the case at the moment. A strengthening of the distinction of wholesale–retail would also be useful, allowing wholesale investors (pension funds, unit trusts) to be subject to home country rules, whereas retail investors would be given more protection. Such an objective-driven structure of supervision is discussed below.

In view of the expected effects of EMU on securitisation and integration of capital markets, simplification of the regulatory framework for securities offerings should be urgently considered. The Commission should prepare a text that integrates existing legislation in one single document, simplifies the provisions and updates the requirements in light of recent developments. As discussed above, there is no need for new legislation, but rather for a synthesis of the existing provisions, allowing for a more transparent framework. The European Commission should, secondly, actively examine implementation of the existing provisions by the member states, and initiate infringement procedures where necessary.

Euro capital markets will require further action from authorities to liberalise market regulations and lift anachronistic barriers to cost-efficient trading, settlement and custody of internationally traded European securities. A host of tax and securities regulations still favour the domestic market and institutions in individual EU countries. They create private hunting grounds or artificial monopolies for certain institutions. In certain markets, listing on the national securities market requires processing of transactions through the national Central Securities Depository (CSD) and depositing with the same. Tax exemptions are often only given for orders processed through the national CSDs. If these issues are not tackled, they will be another hindrance to securitisation.

As compared to banking, cooperation in the domain of securities markets is less developed. A proposal for an EU Committee of Securities Supervisors has been deadlocked for the last five years between the European Parliament and the Council on a matter of principle, that is the degree of freedom which the Commission has to interpret a directive (the so-called 'comitology' procedure). The Committee should be in charge of advising the European Commission on changes to be made to the key securities directives. It should be superior to the Commission's Contact Committee of securities supervisors, instituted by the 1979 stock exchange listing directive, which has only very limited powers.

Securities market supervisors did not wait for this bureaucratic feud to be settled and have in the meantime created the Forum of European Securities Commissions (FESCO) between all members of the European Economic Area (EEA). Launched in December 1997, FESCO is an informal network, with a permanent secretariat at the COB (Commission des Opérations en Bourse) in Paris. It aims to enhance the exchange of information between diversely organised national securities commissions, to develop common regulatory standards in areas that are not harmonised by European directives, and to provide the broadest possible mutual assistance to enhance market surveillance and effective enforcement against abuse. It works on a wide range of issues such as accounting, investor protection, transparency and disclosure.

In the October 1998 paper, *Financial Services, Building A Framework for Action*, the European Commission supported the creation of FESCO. It endorsed the need for action to allow the mutual recognition of public offer prospectuses and listing prospectuses, and called for an upgrading of the ISD. Whether a legislative or non-legislative way will be followed for the latter was left in the middle. Some have called the reopening of the ISD discussion a Pandora's box, and have therefore argued in favour of an interpretative communication, as was done with the second banking directive.[17] However, the rapid global evolution of trading systems and the demutualisation of exchanges might make the former route unavoidable, that is to come to a more consistent definition of exchanges. The definitive work programme in this domain was agreed by the Financial Services Policy Group, instituted by the Vienna Council (December 1998), made up of representatives of the finance ministers of the member states (European Commission, 1999).

FESCO members announced a far-reaching multilateral memorandum of understanding on the surveillance of securities activities and the creation of an integrated surveillance authority, FESCOPOL, on 1 February 1999. The objective of the agreement is to create 'a pan-European regulatory framework to provide the broadest possible mutual assistance between the competent authorities of member states of the EEA so as to enhance market surveillance and effective enforcement against financial abuse'.[18] The agreement covers investigations and enforcement of laws regarding insider dealing, disclosure of interests and financial information, competent intermediaries, clearing and settlement, administration and custody of securities. If necessary, joint investigations will be carried out. The memorandum provides for the creation of the network called FESCOPOL, which should ensure that information flows as rapidly across borders as it does domestically.

IMPLICATIONS OF EMU FOR PRUDENTIAL CONTROL

Monetary union is triggering a broad debate on the adequacy of the supervisory framework for financial institutions. Three concerns inform this debate.

First, strong interpenetration of financial markets as a result of EMU poses a challenge to the home country control rule in the supervision of financial institutions in the EU, and to the limited integration and cooperation of supervisory authorities.

Second, the trend towards scale-enlarging and conglomeration in the financial sector, of which EMU itself is a partial cause, raises the question of whether the current institutional set-up for the supervision of financial institutions and markets is indeed adequate for the task.

Third, the transfer of monetary policy-making to the European Central Bank raises the question of what role that institution will play in the area of prudential supervision and financial stability, which in large part remain member state responsibilities.

The European Central Bank has sometimes been characterised more as a monetary policy rule than as a full central bank. The ECB has independent powers to maintain price stability, but financial stability and prudential control remain in the hands of national authorities. It has only an advisory and coordinating role in the prudential supervision of banks, and will promote the smooth operation of payment systems in EMU. By contrast, a full central bank performs all three functions with the aim of maintaining overall economic and financial stability.

Two sets of questions can thus be raised, related to the supervision of financial institutions on the one hand and markets on the other. Will EMU not require more centralised supervision, at least for banks? Will European banks and financial institutions continue to have a clearly discernible home market? Who will act as lender of last resort for truly European financial institutions? Secondly, how will supervision of financial markets be coordinated in EMU? What degree of coordination has been achieved, and what remains to be done?

Before discussing the implications of EMU for prudential control, we first analyse the rationale for prudential control and examine the institutional set-up of control. We then see how this issue was approached in the EU context and how it has been reflected in recent trends in financial sector supervision. Finally, we discuss what should be changed as a result of EMU.

Box 4.2   Statutory Basis of the ECB's Involvement in Prudential Supervision

The relevant provisions for the ECB's involvement in prudential supervision are Arts 105.5–105.6 of the Maastricht Treaty and the ECB Statute's Art. 25. Art. 105.5 assigns a coordinating role to the ECB in prudential supervision, but these duties may be extended by a Council decision. According to 105.4, the ECB needs to be consulted by the Community and the member states on supervisory matters.

Arts 105.5 and 105.6 of the EU Treaty read:

105.5. The ESCB shall contribute to the smooth conduct of policies pursued by the competent authorities relating to the prudential supervision of credit institutions and the stability of the financial system.

105.6. The Council may, acting unanimously on a proposal from the Commission and after consulting the ECB and after receiving the assent of the European Parliament, confer upon the ECB specific tasks concerning policies relating to the prudential supervision of credit institutions and other financial institutions with the exception of insurance undertakings.

Art. 25 of the statutes of the ECB reads:

25.1. The ECB may offer advice and be consulted by the Council, the Commission and the competent authorities of the member states on the scope and implementation of Community legislation relating to the prudential supervision of credit institutions and to the stability of the financial system.

According to article 105.4 of the Treaty, the ECB needs to be consulted on any proposed act of the Community or member states in its field of competence. This was interpreted by Council decision 98/415/EC of 29 June 1998 as including, amongst others, 'rules applicable to financial institutions insofar as they materially influence the stability of financial institutions and markets'.

The Rationale for Prudential Supervision

The functional division in the supervision of financial institutions has traditionally been based on the differences in risk factor for banks, investment firms and insurance companies. Regulation at the retail level is valid for all three sectors. Consumers are not in a position to judge the safety and soundness of the institutions with which they are dealing, because of imperfect information (agency problems), which raises a public policy issue. Systemic risk was seen as an issue for banks, to a lesser extent for investment firms, and, in principle, not for insurance companies and mortgage banks (which refinance on a long-term basis).

Banks transform liquid short-term liabilities (deposits) into illiquid long-term assets (commercial loans). The deposits can be easily withdrawn, whereas the loans are not readily marketable. A bank can afford this asymmetry as long as withdrawals by depositors take place randomly over time and assets are held to term. In the event of a loss of confidence in the solvency of a bank, however, depositors are faced with a prisoner's dilemma (Goodhart, Hartmann, Llewellyn et al, 1997). While they stand to gain more, collectively, by agreeing to refrain from withdrawals and allowing the bank to realise its assets, their individual interest lies in withdrawing their own deposit first, while the bank is still able to pay. Faced with this situation, a bank can only realise its assets by accepting a discount on the book value of its loans, or worse, can be confronted with a growing proportion of bad loans, which would trigger the insolvency of the bank.

The failure of one bank can have contagious effects on other banks. A run on one bank can lead to a run on all banks, or can have repercussions on the interbank market and the payment and settlement system, thereby endangering the stability of the financial system. The failure of one bank to respect its commitments will immediately affect its creditors. In such situations, central banks should stand by and be ready to inject extra liquidity into the financial system to alleviate temporary liquidity constraints on banks and prevent a crisis from becoming systemic. They should act in close cooperation with banking supervisors, to judge the creditworthiness of a particular bank. In the event that the bank is judged illiquid but not insolvent, lender-of-last-resort support should be provided. Banks contribute to economic efficiency by allocating savings to productive investments, and confidence in this function should be maintained. However, excessively explicit support may stimulate moral hazard, that is, the incentive to take higher risks than normal, thereby reducing prudence in risk management.[19] This was exemplified in the US with the savings and loan crisis at the end of the 1980s, when 1,142 savings and loan associations and 1,395 banks went bankrupt, mainly as a result of maturity mismatching and imprudent lending (9.1% of the total number of banks failed in the period 1980–1994, representing 9.0% of total bank assets). The Swedish financial crisis of the early 1990s is a more recent example of this phenomenon.

To withstand sudden market pressures the Basle Committee, the international organisation of banking supervisors, agreed in 1988 that a minimum solvency ratio of 8% was required (see box 1.2). This rule was implemented for the EU in the 1989 solvency ratio directive. A good solvency ratio, however, is a necessary but not a sufficient condition to ensure a bank's soundness. Much more thus comes into play: the management and structure of the bank, the internal control system, the lending procedures and loan portfolio, and so on. A synthesis of such key issues for bank control was recently published by the Basle Committee, entitled *The Core Principles of Banking Supervision* (September 1997), in response to calls from the G-7 to strengthen financial control at global level. The definition of the solvency ratio itself also contains weaknesses, such as the weighting categories (a zero risk weighting for loans to *all* OECD countries, compared to 100% for all commercial loans), and the overall low level of tier one capital. It is therefore being revised by the G-10.

At the retail level, depositors in banks and investment firms are protected through deposit protection schemes. By protecting deposits, regulators reduce the likelihood of a bank run and increase the stability of the financial system. Depositor protection, however, is comparatively recent in Europe. It was instituted in most member states only in the 1970s, compared to 1933 in the US, and was still non-existent in Greece and Portugal when it became obligatory following the EU's 1992 deposit guarantee schemes directive. The directive introduces a minimum level of protection on deposits of 20,000 ECU and brings it under the responsibility of the home country. In the EU, the home country, which is in charge of controlling the banks under its supervision, is also in charge of guaranteeing its depositors (albeit with a non-export provision and a top-up clause). The same principles and levels of consumer protection were recently introduced through the investor compensation schemes directive for retail clients of investment firms.

Formally, the nature of risk in the investment business is different from that in banking. The assets of investment firms (investment bankers, brokers, fund managers) mainly comprise marketable securities, which are quoted and transacted every day. The asymmetry of contracts that exists in the banking sector does not arise in the investment sector, and thus the susceptibility to a loss of confidence is less high in the latter sector. It is becoming increasingly difficult to use this argument, however. The risk profile of investment firms has changed with the practice of trading in derivative instruments, where the risk exposure can be much higher than in the primary business and can change rapidly. Investment banks are also big players in many large-value transactions in the financial system. The failure of one large investment bank or fund manager could thus impact on the whole financial system and have systemic effects, as could recently be noticed in South-East Asia, or as was argued in favour of the LTCM-rescue. Finally, investment banking has become increasingly fused with traditional banking business, certainly in Europe, where universal banking was taken as the model in the second banking directive.

In the insurance sector, the risk of systemic effects through the insolvency of one company does not occur, except for connected undertakings with large intragroup exposures. The failure of one insurance company should not lead to a run on insurance companies to withdraw policies. As compared to bank deposits, policies are illiquid claims that are transformed into liquid assets. On the life-side of the business, policies are held until a pre-defined date of maturity, and contributions are set on the basis of the mortality statistics. On the non-life side, contributions are defined on the basis of accident statistics, or other variables.

Prudential supervision in insurance is mainly a matter of controlling the asset–liability match. Liabilities of insurance companies are backed by technical reserves, mostly readily marketable assets, established to cover future claims from the policies underwritten. Rules on the prudential asset spread are defined in the EU's third insurance directives. In addition, insurance companies are required to hold a certain amount of additional resources for unexpected losses, the solvency margin, and to reinsure their claims with reinsurance companies. According to a recent Commission report, this system has worked well: over the last 20 years, only a few cases of deficiencies of insurance companies were observed in the European Economic Area (EEA). A significant proportion of these could be remedied through a capital increase or by a takeover by other insurance undertakings, thus avoiding final insolvency and winding-up.[20]

Three factors could render insurance companies (and also mortgage banks) more prone to systemic risk: (i) elements of consumer protection law which allow consumers to withdraw policies easily (and before maturity), or regulation which requires a guaranteed nominal rate of return on life insurance policies, as is set by legislation in most EU member states; (ii) macro-economic instability, deflation and meltdown of assets, as is the case in Japan; (iii) the emergence of *bancassurance* firms and integrated financial conglomerates. In the case of the two first factors, systemic risk would be provoked by bad government policies, but the latter factor is, within a European perspective, the most critical for regulators at present. While both entities of a bank insurance firm are separately authorised and controlled, supervisory authorities could be unaware of the overall risk profile of the group. The risks at group level do not necessarily equal the sum of the risks of the different entities of the group: the group might have large exposures that do not exist at the entity level. The danger of double gearing of capital or uncontrolled intragroup transactions to cover losses on the one side with gains from the other, also arises. International and European authorities are considering these problems, but no legislation as yet exists at European level.[21]

In banking, on the other hand, the evidence of and proneness to systemic risk is less clear-cut than before. On the basis of empirical research, Kaufman (1995, 1996) shows that there is little solid proof of systemic risk in US banking. Insolvencies at one bank have rarely caused insolvencies at others. Bank failures result from bad management and economic downturns, but banks do not fail in dominos. Shareholders as well as depositors have been able to successfully differentiate financially strong from financially weak banks. According to Kaufman, bank fragility was increased by government policies, not decreased, and has thus become an element of government failure, rather than market failures. Regulators should not concentrate on solving liquidity problems, which induce moral hazard behaviour, but focus on the risks to the macroeconomy.

Secondly, the asymmetry in the asset–liability structure is slowly diminishing, with the proportion of commercial loans to non-banks in total bank assets declining, while marketable securities are increasing. In France, Germany and the UK, the share of securities on the balance sheet doubled over the last ten years to about 20% in 1996 (OECD, 1998). The process of asset securitisation is widely expected to be further stimulated in EMU. Moreover, the ECB has also included illiquid loans in its list of eligible assets for monetary policy operations. The blurring of boundaries in the financial services sector is thus not only applicable on the product side, but also on the risk side, which has important implications for the institutional set-up of supervision.

The Institutional Set-up

In several countries, the institutional structure of prudential control has become a policy issue. Increasing emphasis is being given to the general question of whether the efficiency of regulation and supervision might be influenced by a particular institutional structure. A particular structure might cause an unnecessary duplication of regulatory activity and hence impose a cost on firms and society, or it might miss some aspects of supervision altogether.

As regards banking, the discussion centres on whether all banking supervision needs to be under the same roof of the central bank. The increasing tendency towards conglomeration in the financial services industry is an argument in favour of a single supervisory authority, but the differences in risk profile of the various types of business plead for the opposite. Conglomeration might also strengthen the arguments for more supervision by the objectives of regulation.

Central Bank or Separate Banking Supervisor

Monetary policy and banking supervisory functions are separated in one half of the Community countries and combined in the other half. Generally speaking, the arguments in favour of combining both functions revolve around the fact that it is the central bank's role (in all EU countries) to ensure the stability of the financial system and prevent contagious systemic crises. The performance of bank supervisory and regulatory functions by the central bank should contribute to better control of overall financial stability. Through its role as lender-of-last-resort (LOLR), the central bank should, it is argued, be involved in supervision as well. At the same time, however, this raises an argument against combining both functions. A conflict of interest might arise. The central bank's participation in bank rescues might endanger price stability and increase moral hazard. It might create competitive distortions if central bank money is allocated at preferential rates to a bank in trouble as compared to other banks. Finally, it might raise the expectation in the private sector that the central bank would be influenced by considerations of financial system stability when determining monetary policy. The central bank's reputation might then be at stake.

The fact that both regimes are equally represented in the EU shows that there are no definitive arguments for either model (see Table A1.11). According to Goodhart and Schoenmaker (1995), the question of the appropriate design has to be approached in the context of the particular financial or banking structure of each country rather than as an abstract problem to be solved. An analysis of bank failures over the last two decades showed there to be a much higher frequency of failures in countries with a separated regime than in those with a combined one. This should not, however, lead immediately to the conclusion that the latter regime is better. Many other factors come into play, such as the quality of supervision, the willingness of governments to let a bank fail or the existence of oligopolies in banking. Goodhart and Schoenmaker also find a stronger likelihood of commercial banks being involved in bank rescues in a combined regime, but they see this as a diminishing possibility.

There is, however, a general trend among central banks to retreat from supervisory functions. This was exemplified recently in the UK by the breakaway of the supervisory functions from the Bank of England in May 1997 and the establishment of the Financial Services Authority (FSA), a single financial supervisory authority (see Box 4.3). Several reasons can be advanced for this trend. First, banking is becoming an increasingly complex and less clearly defined business. Leading banks are active in several jurisdictions as providers of a whole series of financial services. Linked to this are new developments in financial supervision, which increasingly emphasise the role of self-regulation and internal risk management in financial institutions. Finally, there is increasing acceptance that the government, not the central bank, should take responsibility for ultimate financial support. The ability of central banks to organise and coordinate bank rescues has been slipping, and bank rescues have become more expensive, going beyond the sums which the central bank can provide from its own resources. This was demonstrated earlier this decade in Norway and Sweden, but also more recently in France. There has consequently been no alternative but to rely on taxpayer funding, leading to more demand for political control of supervisory functions. Close cooperation between the supervisors and the central bank is required, however, since only the central bank

---

Box 4.3   The UK Financial Services Authority

After only a few weeks in office, the new Labour government announced far-reaching changes to the financial regulatory system in the UK. Several bank failures (BCCI, Barings) and fraud scandals (personal pensions) had brought increased public criticism of the UK's financial regulatory system, which was based on a mixture of statutory legislation and a quasi-private system of self-regulatory organisations (SROs). All financial supervisory tasks are now concentrated in the Financial Services Authority (FSA), a fully statutory system of regulation. According to its initiators, the reform should bring about greater coordination and consistency across different areas of regulation, simplified access to the regulator for consumers, clearer lines of accountability and greater efficiency achieved through economies of scale.

The FSA combines banking supervision (formerly the province of the Bank of England), securities (formerly the Securities and Investment Board, SIB) and insurance regulation (formerly the Department of Trade and Industry, DTI). The reform abolished three self-regulatory organisations: the Securities and Futures Authority (SFA), the Investment Management Regulatory Organisation (IMRO) and the Personal Investment Authority (PIA). The FSA will also absorb the powers of the Building Societies Commission and the Friendly Societies Commission. The FSA has rule-making powers and cooperates with exchanges and clearing houses. It is accountable to the government and to Parliament.

The Bank of England remains responsible for ensuring the overall stability of the financial system, which involves monitoring and, when necessary, intervening in the market. A Memorandum of Understanding between the Treasury, the Bank of England and the FSA divides the responsibilities of the different bodies. It establishes a standing committee between these three groups to discuss financial stability and an information-sharing agreement between the Bank and the FSA.

can provide immediate liquidity to the market in case of trouble, and price stability cannot be achieved without financial stability.

Single Financial Supervisor or Specialist Supervisors

Once the question of central bank versus separate banking supervisor has been settled, a second question to be addressed is whether financial supervision should be assigned to one entity or should be determined by the type of business of the institutions under supervision (Box 4.4). The case for the former seems obvious, and was illustrated above in the case of the UK's FSA. It presupposes that there are economies of scale (and probably economies of scope) in supervision, as well as some practical and political advantages. There is one-stop shopping for authorisations for conglomerate financial groups. Expertise is pooled and cooperation between the different functional supervisors is guaranteed. A single authority could also lead to lower supervisory fees, at least in those countries where the financial sector contributes directly to the cost of supervision.

The differences in risk profiles and in the nature of the businesses remain an important argument against a single supervisor, most importantly for banking as compared to the insurance business. In fact, it is doubtful whether a single authority would be more efficient (see Goodhart et al, 1997). A single authority could quickly become a collection of separate divisions. Moreover, it would be a very powerful entity and could increase moral hazard, that is it could reduce the incentive for financial institutions to manage their business prudently. The public perception could emerge that the whole financial sector was under control, and the loss of confidence as a result of the failure of one institution would be even larger.

A specialist supervisor could be closer to the business, more specialised and better aware of the problems of the sector. It could also be more effective and easier to manage. Two other arguments stand out: a growing need for specialisation in supervision and interagency competition. Monitoring potentially dangerous exposures in increasingly globalised financial markets, validating statistical models in a bank's value-at-risk models, supervising complex financial groups, or tracking market behaviour of investment funds require very distinct skills of supervisors, and a large degree of specialisation. It is not assured that these matters can be better controlled in a single supervisor than in specialised supervisors. The second argument, interagency competition, is relevant, although often difficult to advance. Where several agencies work side by side, institutional competition can work and create incentives for each agency to work efficiently (von Hagen 1998). An example is the US structure of banking supervision, where banks can be state or nationally-chartered.

Box 4.4   The Case for

A Single Financial Supervisor	**Specialist Supervisors**
• One-stop shopping for authorisations • Pooling of expertise and economies of scale (certain units could be merged, e.g., authorisations) • Lower supervisory fees (?) • Adapted to evolution in financial sector towards financial conglomerates • Cooperation between type of financial business guaranteed; one lead supervisor for conglomerates • No regulatory arbitrage, regulatory neutrality • More transparent to consumers	• More effective and easier to manage • Clearly defined mandates • More adapted to the differences in risk profiles and nature of the respective financial business, clear focus on objectives and rationale of regulation • Closer to the business • Better knowledge of the business • Lower profile • Stimulates interagency competition

An overview of financial sector supervision in the EU and the rest of Europe shows that three EU countries (Denmark, Sweden and the UK) as well as Norway have a single financial services authority. In some of these countries (as also recently in Japan and South Korea), the integration of supervision resulted from important financial sector trouble or serious oversights in surveillance. In Belgium, the Netherlands and Ireland, the creation of a single authority is either on the political agenda or close to being completed. In the other countries, a broad mixture of systems exists, ranging from separate supervisors to combined banking-and-securities or combined securities-and-insurance supervisors (see Table A1.12).

To complete the overview, it should be noted that a varying degree of institutionalised self-regulation exists in the financial sector in the EU. It was clear in the former supervisory regime in the UK, with the Self-Regulatory Organisations (SROs) SIB, IMRO and SFA (see Box 4.3). Self-regulation in the financial sector is most widespread in the area of securities supervision, where the powers exercised by the stock exchange as compared to the statutory supervision by the securities commission differ importantly across EU countries, and distort rapid comparisons.

The debate on a single versus a specialist regulator often bypasses the key issue, namely, the exchange of information between the different supervisors and the appointment of a lead supervisor. As the problem also rises at the international level, the emergence of financial conglomerates calls for a good exchange of information between the specialist supervisors concerning the risk exposure in the different parts of the group and agreement on a 'lead supervisor', that is, an authority that takes final responsibility for supervising the group. There is no guarantee that a single-authority eases this process. To quote a Bank of England official: 'It is tempting to think that all regulatory questions can be resolved by the creation of a single regulator. Even with everything under one roof, regulatory problems can be resolved efficiently only by close cooperation between regulators, whether they wear different institutional labels or simply different divisional labels within the same regulatory institution'.[22] Different entities with clearly defined responsibilities might be just as effective.

Supervision by Objective

A possible outcome of the conglomeration trend is that supervision will become more objective-driven, since the functional divisions of the business will be increasingly difficult to make. As the differences in risk profiles in the financial sector become less clear to distinguish, and also since risk management within large groups has converged across both bank and non-bank activities, supervision should adjust accordingly, and tilt towards a horizontal model, driven by objectives of regulation.

Financial supervision could be carried out separately by one agency for systemic stability, by a second for minor prudential supervision, and by a third for consumer protection and conduct-of-business considerations. Conduct-of-business supervision looks after transparency, disclosure, fair and honest practices, and equality of market participants. The 'stability' agency should concentrate on systemic problems, the prudential agency controls the solvency and soundness of financial institutions and enforces depositor protection. Such a structure was instituted in Australia, further to the Wallis Committee of Inquiry (1997), which advised that the regulatory system had to facilitate market developments and therefore proposed a triple structure. The Australian Prudential Regulatory Authority (APRA) supervises financial institutions on prudential grounds, the Reserve Bank of Australia looks after systemic stability and provides liquidity assistance, and the Australian Securities and Investment Commission (ASIC) controls market integrity and conduct-of-business rules. APRA and ASIC report to the Treasury. Some EU countries have elements of an objective-driven system of supervision. In Italy, for example, the Banca d'Italia is in charge of controlling financial institutions on financial stability and prudential grounds, while the CONSOB enforces conduct of business rules for the banking and securities industry.

A schematic overview of the objectives of supervision and their importance per type of financial business is given in Table 4.3. Banking and securities are given as one, in view of the universal banking model in Europe. Systemic risk is considered to be a lesser problem in insurance than in banking and securities business. Control of solvency is equally important for both

Table 4.3 *An institutional framework for financial market control*

Type of business/ Objective of supervision	Banking–Securities		Insurance
Systemic risk		xx	x
Prudential (solvency control)		xx	xx
Consumer protection/	Retail	Wholesale	xx
Conduct of business	xx	x	

Note: xx = very important; x = of lesser importance.

sectors. An advantage of supervision by objective is that a distinction can be made between retail and wholesale business in the banking and securities sector, and probably also in insurance. The asymmetry of information and the implications of market failures are much greater in the retail sector, as will be the demand for consumer protection.

From this point of view, it could be argued that the wholesale business would certainly not be better off under a single authority, contrary to what is often asserted. The result of a single supervisory authority would be that the different objectives of supervision were merged and would later disappear, which could ultimately lead to more regulation, including for the wholesale business. This fear has already been raised in recent reports on the UK's FSA, since the distinction retail/wholesale had disappeared in the draft financial services and markets bill (July 1998).[23]

The International Dimension

Recent international bank failures and financial problems have highlighted the global interdependence of financial markets and the need for solutions at that level. The collapse of the British Barings Bank (February 1995) was caused by uncovered positions taken by one trader in Singapore, leading to a loss of $1.4bn. The Japanese firm Daiwa incurred a loss of $1.1bn as a result of fraudulent transactions by a trader in its New York branch (August 1995). The size and repercussions of these losses has induced the G-7 to discuss the issue at all its recent meetings. The Halifax G-7 meeting (June 1995) called for an integrated approach to potential systemic risks and for closer international cooperation in the regulation and supervision of financial institutions and markets. The G-7 invited the Basle Committee on Banking Supervision and IOSCO (International Organisation of Securities Commissions) to work closely together to address the major issues in this area, to examine desirable solutions for the problems identified and to report back.

The Lyon G-7 communiqué (June 1996) focused on the challenges posed to supervisors by financial innovations, the growing phenomenon of cross-border capital movements and the increasing number of internationally active firms. It called for enhanced cooperation among supervisors of global firms, clarification of their roles and improved risk management and transparency in markets. The G-7 Finance Ministers issued a companion report that lent support to the proposals of the Basle Committee and IOSCO for international cooperation and information exchange between banking and securities supervisors through the appointment of a lead supervisor for globally active firms. It lent support to the Joint Forum on financial conglomerates, comprised of banking, securities and insurance supervisors, which agreed on ways to enhance cooperation and to organise the supervision of complex groups. The Joint Forum agreed that supervisors must have the powers to obtain adequate information on the ownership and management structure, and, if necessary, to prohibit structures that hinder effective supervision. And it encouraged private sector efforts to enhance market transparency, to improve reporting and disclosure of derivatives activities, and to expand cooperation among exchanges and securities supervisors for information-sharing arrangements.

In response to the G-7 calls, the Basle Committee on Banking Supervision issued a consultative paper on 'Core Principles for Effective Banking Supervision' in April 1997. The paper was submitted to the G-7 Denver summit (June 1997) and formally published in September 1997.

In the Amendment to the Basle Capital Accord to Incorporate Market Risk, reached by the Basle Committee in 1995, supervisors may allow banks, under certain conditions, to use internal risk-measurement models (value-at-risk (VAR) models). This agreement signalled an important change in the thinking about risk control in banking. For the first time, banks were authorised to use their own risk-control models to determine the minimum regulatory capital that is required to guard against market risk. This move originates from the realisation that formal rules are increasingly cumbersome tools by which to capture market risk, since a bank's risk exposure can change very quickly with its investments. The supervisory authorities set the risk parameters and validate the statistical models. Banks can calculate the VAR against which capital must be held. The VAR estimates potential future losses in a given portfolio within a certain time horizon through fluctuations in interest rates, exchange rates, equity and commodity prices. The Amended Basle Accord became fully effective at the end of 1997 and was incorporated into EU legislation through an amendment to the capital adequacy directive for investment firms and credit institutions (CAD II).

The emphasis on internal models has recently been taken a step further in the US with the 'pre-commitment' approach, which devises an incentive contract between banks and their regulators. It stipulates that a bank or investment firm has to pre-commit to its regulator not to exceed a certain portfolio loss over a certain period. This pre-commitment approach, which should be determined using the institution's own internal VAR models, is at the same time its regulatory market risk capital requirement. If it violates this commitment, then it faces a regulatory penalty.

As recent bank failures have shown, however, even the best models cannot substitute for sound risk-management practices. The Group of Thirty, a Washington-based finance think tank, recommended in a recent report that global institutions and supervisors should work jointly to ensure the safety and efficiency of the international financial system and to prohibit the occurrence of systemic shocks (Group of Thirty, 1997). With increasing volumes and speed of transactions in financial markets, the interdependence of markets is growing and disruptions in the financial system could have more far-reaching effects than in the past. The Group of Thirty therefore proposed the establishment of procedures to contain such crises. As major participants in the large-value payment system, large internationally active banks have a special responsibility in this respect: they should be well capitalised and have management systems that are global in scope and of high standards. Market participants, on the other hand, should be able to judge the risk exposures and controls of such firms, which are difficult to obtain at the moment. National supervisors have difficulty in achieving a global view of such firms, which act beyond their borders and jurisdiction. Global supervision remains a challenge.

The Group therefore recommended a two-pronged approach:

1. Global banks must take the lead and establish a standing committee to develop global principles for managing risk. Such a risk-management framework should cover all aspects of risk monitoring and management and provide the basis for evaluating the firm's own operations and those of major counterparts. These management systems must be submitted to a global audit. Risk exposure should be disclosed on a global, consolidated basis.
2. Supervisors should pursue stronger international cooperation. They should agree on a lead supervisor for global firms, apply a global framework for management controls and set consistent reporting requirements. They should also establish performance criteria and risk-management guidelines for exchanges, clearing houses and settlement systems to strengthen the underpinnings of the entire international system.

The Implications of EMU and the Role of the ECB

EMU should lead to a further quantum step in the integration of European financial markets. Notwithstanding five years of the single market, financial markets have remained fairly isolated. Different currencies have kept the local markets protected from foreign competition. Furthermore, a strong home bias can be noticed. Public debt is largely issued on the local market and is domestically held. Institutional investors are strongly biased towards the local market and are not internationally diversified. Cross-border banking penetration is still very limited. This home bias is confirmed in the analysis of balance sheets of European banks with global ambitions, such as ING, ABN-AMRO or Deutsche Bank. In each case, about 50% or more of the income and profits are generated in the local market, while the European share is still limited (see Table I.1).

The EU regulatory framework, which is based on the system of home country control, is adapted to this situation of limited cross-border activity. The home country supervisors are in charge of controlling the operations of the financial institution throughout the Community. The home country would also be in charge of organising rescue operations for its domestic banks, be it via liquidity support by the central bank, with the assistance of other commercial banks, or, if necessary, with government funds. In the event that the latter route is followed, it will need to comply with the EU's state aid rules.

The limited ECB mandate is in line with the single market framework, and coincides with the trend of withdrawal of supervisory functions in central banking. Involvement of the ECB in bank supervision could force it to assist banks in trouble, which could be difficult to reconcile with the task of maintaining price stability and could compromise its independence. More centralisation of functions other than those essentially required for the execution of joint monetary policy would also have been difficult to realise, as this would go against the subsidiarity principle. Bank supervision can be better executed at the local level, because of the availability of specific expertise of the local market and the limited integration of European financial markets.

But will this framework face EMU? Monetary union will bring great changes in the structure of European financial markets. The euro is the domestic currency in 11 member states. Competition will increase, margins will go down, and further scale increases will be required by banks and financial institutions to remain competitive. This is anticipated by the financial sector in the current restructuring and rationalisation process, which often crosses national and sectoral boundaries. Assets will be held more cross-border in EMU. Since all public debt is denominated in euros, and currency-matching rules in insurance regulation have become meaningless, fixed income investments will be spread over debt of different countries, which will also be prudentially sound, and yields will be measured as compared to a Euro-bond index. Returns on equity investments will be measured against euro equity indexes. Financial market integration can thus be expected to make a quantum step.

Stronger competition in EMU could intensify bank fragility, but the shock absorbers which European banks have are limited. Average profitability of European banks is low, as compared to US commercial banks. Return on assets of all European banks, measured as profit before tax as percentage of total assets, stands at about 0.5% for the period 1994–1996, as compared to 1.75% for the US commercial banks (see Table A1.6). Some countries are doing much better than the EU average, such as the UK and Dutch banks, but in others, such as France, the situation is problematic, with a return on assets of 0.2% in 1996. The concentration wave in the financial sector does not immediately change this situation: merging two weak institutions will not create one strong one, rather, on the contrary, it could aggravate the 'too big to fail' problem. Also supervision will consequently need to make a huge step forward.

A first reaction to this situation is to step up cooperation between supervisors and central banks at the European level. Strong communication lines should be established between supervisory authorities at both national and international levels to aggregate exposures of financial groups and exercise consolidated supervision. The present system of supervisory coordination, based on bilateral memoranda of understanding, risks missing certain elements in the picture of European-wide operating groups, and should be supplemented with a more intensified form of cooperation. In a recent statement, the European Shadow Financial Regulatory Committee (ESFRC 1998) proposed that cooperation between supervisors be underpinned by a clear EU-wide agreement on a code of conduct covering supervisory responsibilities and standards in order to avoid misunderstandings, institutional rivalry, and excessive forbearance by national supervisors. Some institution should therefore be in charge of overseeing the web of bilateral memoranda of understanding.

In the recent Framework for Action paper, the European Commission (October 1998) endorsed the need for greater cooperation between supervisory authorities and proposed to contribute to the elaboration of a 'supervisors' charter', setting down relative responsibilities and mechanisms for coordination between supervisors. The Commission also committed itself to cooperate in the review of the Basle capital rules and to examine prudential issues raised by conglomerates. This paper was endorsed by the Vienna European Council (11–12 December 1998), which asked a policy group of special representatives of the Ministers of Finance to report on concrete measures for the Cologne European Council (June 1999).

However, something more might be needed within EMU, as was revealed as a result of the recent financial market crisis. It emerged that the exposure of European banks to emerging markets was more than three times higher than that of North American banks. The aggregate exposure of European banks to Asia, Latin America and Eastern Europe stood at about 400bn ECU at the end of 1997, compared to about 125bn ECU for the North American banks (US and Canada). Moreover, lending of European banks to these regions has increased strongly over the last three years, especially after the first signs of the emerging market crisis became apparent in July 1997 (BIS 1998). European banks have thus actively contributed to the asset bubble in emerging markets. This raises questions about internal risk management within European banks, and about external control on lending policies. No European body was (and still is not) apparently aware of the aggregate exposure of European banks to these regions.

This situation should be seen in the perspective of EMU and the role of the ECB. As indicated before, the ECB is in charge of monetary stability, but not of financial stability, which remains a member state responsibility, together with prudential supervision.[24] This set-up could be characterised as part of the 'constructive ambiguity' (Prati and Schinasi 1998) which is used in the design of safety nets in the banking sector. In order to reduce moral hazard, LOLR procedures in banking were deliberately kept ambiguous. However, this argument is no longer valid. Maintaining a high degree of ambiguity has led to excessive risk taking by financial institutions and too much forbearance by authorities in the face of banking problems. Such policy can only be modified in a climate of greater transparency regarding the support which will be offered to banks in trouble, and under what circumstances (Enoch, Stella and Khamis 1997).

Within the EMU context, the ambiguity of LOLR procedures could, however, rapidly become 'destructive', if national central banks continue to provide liquidity assistance to local problem banks at their own discretion. In EMU, the capacity of national central banks to provide liquidity to local institutions is potentially in conflict with the ECB's responsibility for determining liquidity at EMU level. Any operation that is undertaken on the national level has EMU-wide monetary repercussions. For example, an interest rate subsidy to a local problem bank may in the end be paid for by other banks in the EMU and their customers. For these reasons, and on the grounds of competitive equality, procedures for LOLR operations should be harmonised and responsibility for emergency liquidity provision should be clearly allocated between the ECB and national central banks. The procedures should require adequate collateral (following the ESCB Statute), penal interest rates and, above all, prior authorisation from the ECB for the injection of liquidity at local level. This should be made public and thus contribute to reducing moral hazard.

The problem is that the current Treaty provisions are not sufficiently clear as to whether ECB authorisation is required for local LOLR operations. According to the ESCB statute, national central banks can purchase non-eligible collateral from illiquid institutions on their own responsibility (Art. 14.4), or they can expand the list of eligible tier two collateral.[25] The ECB's Governing Council for its part could prohibit any such operation when it 'interferes with the objectives and tasks of the ESCB' (Art. 14.4) or with the guidelines and instructions issued according to Articles 12.1 and 14.3 of the Statute. The

IMF therefore called upon the ECB to clarify the procedures for LOLR in EMU (IMF 1998: pp. 108–109).

The LOLR issue should not, however, be overemphasised. The 'central bank money solution' to banks in trouble is limited, and has been a rare event in industrial countries over the past decades. Markets and regulation have evolved since Bagehot developed his theory on LOLR. The probability of a bank being solvent, but illiquid, and at the same time lacking sufficient collateral to obtain central bank funding is limited, as Tommaso Padoa-Schioppa, Member of the ECB Board, emphasised in a speech on banking supervision in EMU. More common are the 'private money solution', as with Barings and Long Term Capital Management (LTCM) and the 'taxpayers' money solution', as used with Crédit Lyonnais and Banco di Napoli. The latter solutions are not a matter for central banks, although they may be involved in the rescue. It does, however, also raise a European issue, since the approaches differ across countries, and affect the equality in market participation.

As regards the stability of markets, the current set-up has an implication that nobody is in charge of aggregating and examining exposures in the European banking system to detect signs of potential financial trouble. According to Bini-Smaghi (1998), this information is not available at ECB level which will seriously impede its capacity to assess the extent of liquidity crisis in European markets. The ESFRC (1998) therefore recommended that, within EMU, the current cooperative mechanisms for supervision of institutions will have to be supplemented by a European-wide structure to monitor markets. This reflects the fact that any supervisory shortcomings in a particular jurisdiction would be quickly felt in other member states. The new structure could take the form of a European Observatory of Systemic Risk (Aglietta and de Boissieu 1998). The aim would be to ensure common supervisory and transparency standards, to monitor market developments across Europe and alert national and European authorities to exposures with a potentially systemic impact. This body might or might not be a part of the ECB. In the former case, the legal mechanism exists already, since Art. 105.6 of the Treaty provides for an expansion of the role of the ECB in this domain.

Following the subdivision of supervision along objectives, as discussed above, Table 4.4 summarises the required changes to the current set-up of supervision in the perspective of EMU.

For the time being, the ECB will need to have sufficient resources to make a quick assessment of the situation in the different financial markets. National supervisory authorities will need to transmit information on the exposure of the banking system on a regular basis to the ECB. Opposition of national authorities to sharing information with the ECB will only strengthen and accelerate the emergence of a more centralised supervisory authority in this domain. At ECB level, the establishment of the Banking Supervision Committee within the ECB is a useful step towards information sharing. In contrast to the Commission's Banking Advisory Committee

Table 4.4   *Objectives of supervision and deficiencies in the perspective of EMU*

Objective of supervision	Current set-up	Required changes for EMU
Systemic risk	National supervisory authorities and/or NCBs	Clear role for ESCB/ECB
		Create European Observatory of Systemic Risk
Prudential control (solvency control)	National supervisory authorities (home country)	Strengthen exchange of information: need for multilateral Memoranda of Understanding; intensified cooperation
	Bilateral Memoranda of Understanding	
	Different attitudes to banks in trouble	Draft code of conduct between supervisors
	Excessive forbearance	Align lender-of-last-resort procedures, prior authorisation of ECB
		Harmonise bank exit policies
Consumer protection/ conduct of business	Host country (country where service is provided) for retail and wholesale business	Home country for wholesale business

(BAC) which has a mainly legislative role, the EBSC's tasks fall on the macro-prudential side: to monitor the overall stability of the financial system, to promote the exchange of information between supervisors and give ample warning of new developments.

For Tommaso Padoa-Schioppa, Member of the ECB board in charge of prudential matters, the ECB's Banking Supervision Committee is an embryonic euro area banking supervisor, which can be 'enhanced to the full extent required for banking supervision in the euro area to be as prompt and effective as it is within a single nation'. This Committee will develop the multilateral form of supervision, which has so far been little used in the EU. Padoa-Schioppa also expressed confidence about the coordinating role of the ECB in the area of prudential supervision, which it can exercise on the basis of its advisory role in this domain.[26]

Outlook

It might be as tempting to believe that EMU would call for a single supervisory authority at EU level, as that the conglomeration trend in the financial sector would call for single financial services' supervisors. Many elements must be taken into account in the design of an optimal structure for financial supervision: moral hazard, the objectives of supervision, inter-agency competition, market discipline, efficiency and accountability.

Limiting the ECB functions to monetary policy is part of a general trend of withdrawal from supervisory functions in central banking and fits with the home country control principles of the single market. Specific expertise in and knowledge of prudential control is situated at the local level, where the bulk of the operations of financial institutions is still located, and where the lender-of-last-resort will be provided. Greater centralisation of functions apart from what is essentially required for the execution of joint monetary policy would have been difficult to achieve, as that would violate the principle of subsidiarity. Giving the ECB an explicit LOLR role, as argued by Prati and Schinasi (1998), would also not be desirable, because of the link with fiscal powers (for eventual bank rescues) and the related accountability, which remain at the state level.

However, EMU adds an additional layer to the already complicated structure of financial supervision in the EU, which might reduce consistency and operability, mainly on the systemic side. What needs to be done primarily is to step up cooperation between supervisors at both national and European levels, and institute a hierarchy when it comes to emergency lending and responses to financial stability problems. Although the latter task remains at the local level, it is clearly related to monetary policy. Unlimited lender-of-last-resort support at the local level will spill over into the whole euro area. Price stability cannot be achieved if financial stability is not in place.

It is therefore of the utmost importance to develop firm procedures between national central banks, local supervisors and the ECB to monitor the stability of financial institutions and markets. The ECB will need to be fully informed about developments in local financial markets, to judge whether they might become systemic at the European level. It will at the same time have to make sure that the playing field is levelled for financial institutions in the EU. To avoid misunderstandings and institutional rivalries, the ECB should exploit its position as *primus inter pares* and set common rules in cooperation with the NCBs and the supervisory authorities on the scope of the safety net for financial institutions. These arrangements should, as far as possible, be made public.

As far as the stability of financial markets is concerned, procedures to be followed in times of crises should be agreed. It is, however, clear that, should a generalised liquidity problem emerge at European level, the ECB will be the institution to intervene and to coordinate the response. The creation of a European observatory for systemic risk, close to the ECB, would be extremely useful, to scrutinise developments in European financial markets and to aggregate exposures in the European banking system.

In the area of securities markets, big efforts need to be made by supervisors to match market developments. Although FESCO is now in place, the process of cooperation and coordination is clearly in its infancy. Supervisors will need to make sure that confidence in Europe's capital markets can be maintained, and that the same standards apply across markets.

Supervisors and policy-makers will need to watch closely the effects of financial market integration as a result of EMU, and be prepared to adapt the institutional structure of financial control to market developments. In the longer run, more far-reaching institutional adaptations will be required. Consideration should therefore be given to a more holistic approach to financial supervision, in line with the conglomeration trend in the financial sector. Regulatory objectives will increasingly be difficult to apply on a functional or vertical basis, but need to be assessed across the board. This will also show up where the biggest gaps in efficient supervision exist at European level.

NOTES

1. For more examples, see Price Waterhouse, *Corporate Taxes, A Worldwide Summary* (1997).
2. The third element of the package constitutes a commitment on the abolition of withholding taxes on interest and royalty payments between companies forming part of a group. A first proposal on the subject was presented in 1990. The new proposal was adopted by the European Commission on 4 March 1998 (COM (1998) 67 final). For the 1 December 1997 Ecofin conclusions, see *Official Journal* of the EC, C 2 of 6.1.1998, p. 2.
3. Proposal for a Council Directive to ensure a minimum of effective taxation of savings income in the form of interest payments within the Community, COM(1998)295 of 20 May 1998.
4. The 1988 agreement on the liberalisation of capital movements was linked to a political commitment to harmonise withholding taxes in the Community. A 1989 draft directive provoked severe objections from the UK, Germany and Luxembourg, and had to be withdrawn by the European Commission (Proposal for a

common system of withholding tax on interest income, COM(89)60 of 8.2.1989).

5. See 'Overcoming Accounting Diversity to Integrate Europe's Capital Markets or Why Double Accounting Does Not Pass the Cost/Benefit Test', note presented by John Hegarty to the CEPS Working Party on Capital Markets and EMU, 20 October 1997.
6. European Commission (1995a), *Accounting Harmonisation: A New Strategy vis-à-vis International Harmonisation*, COM(95)508.
7. For a more detailed overview of this debate, see Lannoo (1995, 1999).
8. European Commission (1995b), p. 51.
9. European Commission, Press Release IP/98/1135 of 17 December 1998.
10. This was suggested in 1995 by the CEPS Working Party on Corporate Governance in Europe. See Lannoo (1995).
11. The OECD adopted Corporate Governance Guidelines in the spring of 1999.
12. See Steil (1996: pp. 113–137) for further details on the directive and the negotiations resulting in the compromise.
13. The main supervisory agent is the Commission des Opérations en Bourse (COB), but the Comité des Marchés financiers, a self-regulatory body, is in charge of supervising market transactions.
14. Council Directive 87/345 of 22 June 1987 amending Directive 80/390 coordinating the requirement for the drawing-up, scrutiny, and distribution of the listing particulars to be published for the admission of securities to official stock exchange listing, *OJ* L 185 of 4.7.1987; Council Directive 90/211 of 23 April 1990 amending directive 80/390 in respect of the mutual recognition of public-offer prospectuses as stock exchange listing particulars, *OJ* L 112 of 3.5.1990.
15. Council Directive 89/298 coordinating the requirements for the drawing-up, scrutiny and distribution for the prospectus to be published when securities are offered to the public, *OJ* L 124 of 5.5.1989.
16. Stanislas Yassukovich, 'Single Market for Equities', *Financial Times*, 23.1.98.
17. On 21 December 1998, the European Commission published a report on the operation of certain articles of the investment services directive, on which basis it concluded that there is no need to amend the directive. Only a German suggestion regarding the notification of installation of trading systems in other member states seems to merit further study, it says. See COM(1998)780 final.

18. FESCO, Signature of a European Memorandum of Understanding on the Surveillance of Securities Activities and Creation of FESCOPOL, Press release, 1 February 1999.
19. The term moral hazard comes from the insurance world which focused attention to the problem arising when an insurance company cannot observe whether the insured exerts effort to prevent a loss.
20. European Commission, Report to the Insurance Committee on the Need for Further Harmonisation of the Solvency Margin, COM(97)398, 24.07.97.
21. The Tripartite Group, composed of banking, securities and insurance regulators, published a report on the subject in 1995; in February 1998, the Basle Committee published a report on 'Supervision of Financial Conglomerates'.
22. J. Footman, official of the Bank of England, quoted in Goodhart et al (1997).
23. See Clifford Chance (1998).
24. Art. 105.5 of the Treaty and Art. 25.1 of the ESCB Statute, see Box 4.2.
25. According to the ESCB statute, lending by central banks to commercial banks must be based on adequate collateral, that is marketable paper, such as government bonds. Collateral is subdivided in two tiers: tier one consists of marketable debt instruments which fulfil uniform euro area-wide eligibility criteria specified by the ECB; tier two consists of additional assets, marketable and non-marketable (loans on the books of banks), which are of particular importance for national financial markets and banking systems and for which eligibility criteria are established by national central banks, based on minimum standards set by the ECB.
26. Tommaso Padoa-Schioppa, Banking Supervision in EMU, Speech for the London School of Economics, London, 24 February 1999.

Conclusions

In the first days of 1999, wholesale markets in the EMU area moved to the euro. All of a sudden, there was one single dominant currency in stock, bond, money and derivatives markets in Europe. This changeover is expected to unleash important but difficult-to-forecast dynamic effects, which will differ from sector to sector.

The introduction of the euro had an immediate impact in the money and foreign exchange markets, but change will be slower in other areas. The impact on foreign exchange markets was immediate in the sense that only the euro is now quoted against third currencies. In the interbank market, the impact was also immediate since interbank business is now conducted in euros. But even in this area markets have not totally integrated immediately since local market characteristics survive, for example, in terms of the instruments that are used in different countries.

The main focus of our analysis has been on capital—as opposed to short-term money—markets. In this area, national idiosyncrasies will persist for a longer period. Our analysis suggests that change will be quicker in the markets for fixed income than for equities. The first aspect to change in the bond market is the international dimension as the euro has become the most important currency after the dollar as from January 1999. The international use of the euro is already increasing as both issuers and investors in third countries discover that this is a convenient currency to use. But the domestic dimension is no less important. A larger and more liquid bond market reduces the cost of funding debt both for governments and for the private sector. A unified market for public debt can only arise, however, if investors spread their portfolio across the entire euro area. This is more likely to happen quickly for institutional investors whose performance is likely to be measured against a euro-area-wide benchmark. Large enterprises might find that the larger market makes it more attractive to substitute bank loans with bonds, thus leading to the emergence of a corporate bond market.

In the area of equity markets, integration will take more time because this market is affected much more by differences in taxation, company law and attitudes towards corporate governance. But even here, some consequences can be identified. The move to euro listing in stock markets will lead to a reorientation of trades to a firm's domestic stock exchange. Within the EU, the need for multiple listings will diminish, but the home base of firms and the local stock exchange will remain important for some time to come. Critical mass, efficient marketing and the cost of maintaining the trading software will determine whether smaller exchanges will survive. But the place of trading will continue to matter since many legal rules covering investor protection, settlement or winding-up remain different.

One general thread that runs through our analysis is that Europe is likely to become the home market for institutional investors, but not yet for households. Remaining regulatory differences are likely to be more of a deterrent for households than for institutional investors. This requires action by policymakers, most importantly in the area of taxes, but also in regulations covering securities market issues. Authorities will also need to scrutinise whether the framework for financial market supervision matches financial market integration. Initiatives might be needed to strengthen cooperation between supervisors, and between the supervisors and the European Central Bank, to monitor the stability of financial markets.

It is difficult to predict how quickly the process of integration will be put in train. It is likely that the market-driven forces will take effect in a matter of a few years. Within this time span, one can expect euro-area-wide benchmarks and common instruments to emerge in banking and the bond markets. The rebalancing of portfolios of investors from third countries might take a bit longer. Households in the EU are likely to be the slowest to adjust, but they will react quickly when it comes to spot tax arbitrage opportunities. One should thus expect to see a 'cat and mouse' game being played between public authorities and taxpayers in which the former will constantly try to close the loopholes and iron out inconsistencies in national fiscal regulations. Despite the accelerating pace at which the EU is moving in the fiscal area, this might take some time. But there can be no doubt as to the final outcome.

Appendix 1
Statistical Appendix

Table A1.1 *Comparative data on European Stock Markets (1998)*

Country	Domestic capitalisation 1998 (ECU mn)	(%GDP)	Domestic listed companies	Foreign listed companies	Value of equity trading Domestic	Foreign	Turnover velocity of domestic shares
B	210,941	94.7	156	120	49,831	4,831	24
DK	84,242	53.9	242	12	59,047	1,045	70
D	932,303	48.9	741	2,784	1,241,442	87,612	133
GR	69,483	64.9	229	0	42,006	0	60
E	342,643	69.4	481	5	568,164	1,146	166
F	839,414	65.4	784	178	510,078	10,883	61
IRL	59,365	79.7	78	23	36,704	0	62
I	485,412	46.5	239	4	435,408	511	90
L	32,494	219.6	53	224	1,473	21	5
NL	513,911	152.1	214	145	361,882	1,716	70
AUS	30,484	16.1	96	32	15,236	238	50
P	53,637	56.0	135	0	42,406	0	79
FIN	131,917	119.0	129	2	54,055	113	41
SWE	237,459	116.2	258	18	181,693	23,480	77
UK	1,957,599	156.3	2,399	521	940,486	1,628,273	48
EU 11	3,632,520	62.9	3,106		3,316,679	107,069	91
EU 15	5,981,303	79.8	6,234		4,539,911	1,759,866	76
CH	587,198	238.3	232	193	580,704	29,819	99
N	39,551	30.2	214	22	35,614	2,460	90
JAPAN	2,078,496	62.6	1,838	52	761,900	1,186	37
US-NYSE	8,751,659	116.1	2,278	391	5,727,502	478,281	65
US-NASDAQ	2,150,766	28.5	4,572	438	4,511,246	183,903	210

Notes: Listed companies include main and parallel markets; listed companies and market capitalisation do not include investment trusts, listed unit trusts and UCITS. The data refer to the main market of the states mentioned, except for Germany, where they cover the federation of German exchanges. Turnover figures are only indicative within certain stock exchanges and therefore cannot be used as a reliable basis of comparison between different countries.
Sources: FIBV, FESE and European Commission.

Table A1.2   *Evolution of stock market capitalisation (as % of GDP)*

Country	1993	1995	1996	1997	1998
B	38.9	38.5	46.0	58	94
D	24.3	23.8	28.7	39	49
E	32	34.8	42.3	55	69
F	38.3	33.2	38.9	49	65
I	14.4	19.7	21.7	31	46
NL	61.7	73.9	97.9	133	152
SWE	56.8	76.7	97.5	114	117
UK	128.1	123.2	153.8	194	156
EU 11	29.0	30	36.0	48	63
EU 15	43.2	43.3	53.3	70	80
CH	117.7	131.1	136.1	216	240
JAPAN	75.2	71.4	69.4	54	63
US (2)	84.0	97.5	117.7	160	145

Sources: FIBV and FESE.

Table A1.3   *Domestic listed companies in major EU countries, Switzerland, Japan and the US*

	1975	1980	1985	1990	1995	1998
B	290	225	192	182	150	156
D	471	459	472	413	678	741
E	476	494	334	427	378	481
F	724	586	489	443	710	784
I	152	134	147	220	250	239
NL	242	214	232	260	217	214
SWE	101	103	164	121	212	258
UK	2,820	2,659	2,116	1,946	1,971	2,399
CH	104	118	131	182	216	232
JAPAN	1,398	731	1,476	1,627	1,714	1,838
US NYSE	1,523	1,533	1,487	1,678	1,996	2,278

Note: Figures concern listings on the main market in the country concerned.
Source: FIBV.

Table A1.4 Structural features of general gross government debt (1997)

	Total debt (% GDP)	Domestic ownership (%)	Average maturity (years)	<1 year	1–5 years	>5 years	Of which in foreign currency (%)
B	122.2	—	4.3	24.6	35.7	39.7	7.3
DK	65.1	59.3	5.3	8.1	91.9		13.0
DE*	60.4	71.1	4.7	18.5	81.5		0.0
EL	108.7	76.3	—	13.3	86.7		—
E	68.8	78.5	3.7	30.6	37.2	32.1	9.6
F	58.0	86.7	5.3	29.4	29.5	41.1	7.0
IRL	66.3	—	5.0	8.9	44.8	46.3	26.2
I	121.6	79.0	4.5	49.4	25.8	24.8	6.9
L	6.7	85.1	7.2	0.1	10.1	89.9	0.2
NL	72.1	—	5.5	6.7	30.3	63.0	—
AU	66.1	—	5.9	10.7	40.2	49.1	—
P	62.0	—	3.4	33.1	38.0	28.9	—
SF	55.8	36.8	4.7	19.1	48.1	32.8	49.6
SW	76.6	54.2	2.6	34.0	66.0		31.7
UK	53.4	82.4	10.1	26.8	73.2		3.5

Sources: EMI (1998), data for Germany are 1996.

Table A1.5   *Key data on European banking (1996)*

	Inhabitants per branch	Bank employment as % of total employment	Gross income as % of GDP	Gross income per employee (1,000 ECU)
B	567	2.11	5.8	156.7
DK	2,382	1.71	4.2	129.6
DE	1,880	2.10	4.5	117.3
EL	6,614	1.11	2.7	59.5
E	1,060	1.95	5.9	112.6
F	2,220	1.86	4.9	146.3
I	2,675	1.64	4.8	140.8
IRL	2,375	2.53	7.3	126.2
L	1,210	9.45	39.4	256.4
NL	2,277	1.69	7.1	190.6
AU	1,721	1.92	6.4	162.3
P	2,620	1.37	6.1	84.6
SF	3,634	1.30	3.8	137.9
SW	3,545	1.07	3.9	182.4
UK	3,525	1.94	4.7	101.0
EU 15	1,986	1.86	5.0	128.2
USA	3,740	1.37	4.1	134.9
J	8,561	0.59	1.8	172.5
CH	1,967	3.06	10.8	222.1

Sources: OECD (1998) and national data; Greece and Japan only include commercial banks.

Table A1.6 *Profitability in banking*

	Return on equity					Return on assets				
	1985	1990	1993	1995	1996	1985	1990	1993	1995	1996
B	13.4	8.3	14.1	12.9	15.3	0.34	0.28	0.36	0.33	0.39
DK	34.2	−3.3	10.6	18.5	16.1	2.96	−0.26	0.58	1.28	1.11
DE	19.1	11.9	13.6	12.6	12.3	0.68	0.45	0.54	0.53	0.50
EL		20.8	21.6	24.4	16.7		0.81	0.98	1.14	0.75
E	10.1	13.6	3.8	9.2	9.7	0.79	1.25	0.33	0.79	0.84
F		10.1	2.9	3.6	4.8		0.34	0.13	0.16	0.20
IRL				20.2	20.4				1.36	1.36
I		12.2	8.8	3.7	5.1		0.91	0.75	0.34	0.46
L	9.5	6.7	19.9	19.9	22.3	0.33	0.22	0.50	0.50	0.55
NL	19.5	12.3	15.9	17.0	17.6	0.73	0.49	0.65	0.71	0.72
AU		8.6	8.7	8.1	9.6		0.40	0.44	0.38	0.42
P	5.4	12.5	9.2	7.7	7.7	0.30	1.38	0.88	0.63	0.64
SF	5.6	5.6	−28.4	−7.9	8.0	0.36	0.39	−1.43	−0.38	0.42
SW	4.8	3.1	4.5	21.5	24.3	0.31	0.18	0.26	1.35	1.30
UK	24.2	14.4	19.3	28.6	25.6	1.09	0.69	0.73	1.11	1.07
EU 11		11.3	8.2	8.4	9.3		0.53	0.42	0.42	0.46
EU 15		10.9	9.0	10.0	10.9		0.54	0.41	0.63	0.53
USA	14.0	10.7	21.2	21.6	21.6	0.86	0.69	1.69	1.75	1.78
J	19.0	11.3	5.0	−5.0	0.8	0.45	0.36	0.19	−0.17	0.03
CH	11.5	7.8	10.5	8.5	1.7	0.70	0.51	0.68	0.54	0.10

Sources: OECD (1998); Greece, Japan and the US only include commercial banks.

Table A1.7   *Assets of insurance companies, pension funds, investment funds and banks (1996) (ECU bn)*

	Insurance cos	GDP %	Pension funds	GDP %	Invest. funds	GDP %	Banks	GDP %
B	59.1	28.3	8.8	4.2	22.0	10.6	688.6	330.3
DK	55.1	40.2	30.6	22.3	7.5	5.5	158.2	115.4
D	530.9	28.5	109.7	5.9	110.1	5.9	3,709.5	198.8
GR	2.0	2.1	2.8	2.9	12.6	13.1	65.0	67.3
E	50.5	11.0	17.8	3.9	114.3	24.8	785.5	170.6
F	460.6	37.9	55.4	4.6	428.1	35.2	2,892.1	237.8
IRL	9.8	14.9	25.6	39.0	43.0	65.3	118.7	180.3
I	122.9	12.9	25.9	2.7	103.7	10.8	1,368.4	143.2
L	6.4	47.5	0.0	0.2	283.0	2,112.2	490.0	3,656.7
NL	138.9	44.9	278.3	90.0	54.0	17.4	816.0	263.7
A	36.2	20.1	2.0	1.1	31.8	17.6	424.5	235.7
P	10.4	12.6	8.3	9.9	12.6	15.1	181.7	218.7
FIN	13.4	13.7	14.3	14.7	2.0	2.1	107.9	110.7
S	119.4	59.8	66.0	33.1	28.3	14.2	212.0	106.2
UK	846.4	94.6	770.8	86.2	159.6	17.8	1,247.3	139.5
EU 15	2,462.1	36.3	1,416.4	20.9	1,412.5	20.8	13,265.4	195.6
CH	172	72.5	191.6	80.8	38.4	16.2	917.9	387.6
US	2,308	41.7	3,867.0	67.5	2,842.7	49.6	3,584.5	62.5
JAPAN	3,865	98.9	NA		337.4	9.3	4,431.0	122.4

Notes
1. Insurance companies in the EU apply different valuation techniques, with Ireland, the Netherlands and the UK applying current value for investments, whereas most other continental European countries use historic value.
2. To the extent that insurance companies and pension funds hold investment funds, there could be some overlap in the amount of assets held by both groups.
Sources: Eurostat, EFRP, FEFSI and OECD (1998a,b).

Table A1.8 *Pension funds asset growth (ECU bn)*

	1992	1993	1994	1995	1996	EU total %
B	4.4	6.2	5.8	7.61	8.8	0.6
DK	16.2	23.3	22.4	23.6	30.6	2.2
D	68.8	94.9	90.1	96.7	109.7	7.7
GR	0.0	0.0	0.0	2.3	2.8	0.2
E	5.2	9.0	9.3	13.7	17.8	1.3
F	28.2	36.8	41.1	50.2	55.4	3.9
IRL	10.9	15.4	17.1	19.8	25.6	1.8
I	7.9	10.4	18.4	22.1	25.9	1.8
L	0.0	0.0	0.0	0.0	0.0	0.0
NL	162.5	234.1	233.2	261.8	278.3	19.6
AU				1.5	2.0	0.1
P	1.8	4.1	5.0	6.1	8.3	0.6
FIN				12.9	14.3	1.0
SWEDEN	35.6			54.0	66.0	4.7
UK	439.7	642.7	574.0	616.4	770.8	54.4
EU	781.1	1,077.0	1,016.3	1,188.7	1,416.4	100.0

Source: EFRP.

Table A1.9 *Investment funds asset growth (ECU bn)*

	1993	1994	1995	1996	1997	EU total %
B	13.6	15.4	18.8	22.0	30.6	1.8
DK	3.9	4.5	5.0	7.5	11.9	0.7
D	70.5	92.1	104.7	110.1	133.7	7.7
GR	3.1	4.6	8.1	12.6	23.5	1.4
E	64.6	70.1	78.3	114.3	161.6	9.3
F	433.9	406.5	406.8	428.1	454.5	26.1
IRL	4.7	6.4	6.6	43.0	43.0	2.5
I	57.7	65.4	62.4	103.7	175.0	10.0
L	222.2	231.4	253.3	283.0	342.8	19.7
NL	44.2	39.0	48.6	54.0	52.4	3.0
A	16.3	19.2	26.1	31.8	40.8	2.3
P	8.4	10.5	10.4	12.6	13.5	0.8
FIN	0.0	0.9	0.9	2.0	3.2	0.2
S	22.3	16.5	21.0	28.3	41.7	2.4
UK	117.9	108.9	120.4	159.6	213.3	12.2
EU	1,083.3	1,091.3	1,171.5	1,412.5	1,741.5	100.0
CH	30.6	31.8	35.0	38.4	48.9	2.8
US				2,842.7	3,953.0	

Source: FEFSI.

Table A1.10   *Investment funds asset spread in the EU (1997) (ECU bn)*

	Total	Equity funds	% of total	Bond funds	% of total	Mixed funds	% of total	Money market funds	% of total
B	30.6	14.1	46.1	6.4	21.1	8.6	28.1	1.4	4.7
DK	11.9	5.4	45.5	6.3	53.1	0.2	1.4	0.0	0.0
D	133.7	50.6	37.9	64.4	48.2	3.8	2.8	14.8	11.1
EL	23.5	0.8	3.2	6.5	27.5	2.0	8.5	14.3	60.8
E	161.6	16.9	10.5	66.2	40.9	17.9	11.1	60.7	37.5
F	454.5	61.9	13.6	123.7	27.2	85.1	18.7	183.8	40.4
IRL	43.0	13.0	30.2	13.0	30.2	14.0	32.6	3.0	7.0
I	175.0	37.5	21.4	80.4	45.9	11.4	6.5	45.6	26.1
L	342.8	87.1	25.4	163.6	47.7	22.9	6.7	69.1	20.2
NL	52.4	28.2	53.9	15.9	30.2	3.0	5.7	5.3	10.1
A	40.8	3.0	7.3	27.7	67.8	10.2	25.0	0.0	0.0
P	13.5	1.5	11.2	4.9	36.0	2.9	21.3	4.2	31.5
FIN	3.2	1.0	31.8	0.6	18.4	0.7	21.4	0.9	28.3
S	41.7	32.3	77.4	4.2	10.1	5.2	12.5	0.0	0.0
UK	213.3	183.1	85.8	13.1	6.1	16.2	7.6	1.0	0.5
EU	1,741.5	536.4	30.8	596.7	34.3	204.0	11.7	404.3	23.2
CH	48.9	33.2	67.9	15.7	32.1	0.0	0.0	0.0	0.0
US	3,953.0	2,148.4	54.3	778.7	19.7	114.3	2.9	911.7	23.1
JAP	339.1	73.3	21.6	156.0	46.0	12.3	3.6	97.5	28.7

Sources: FEFSI (1997), data for Japan and US are provisional (first 9 months).

Table A1.11 *Monetary and bank supervisory functions in the EU, Switzerland and the US*

	Regime	Monetary agency	Supervisory agency
AU	S	National Bank of Austria (CB)	(Federal) Ministry of Finance (MF)
B	S	National Bank of Belgium (CB)	Banking and Finance Commission
DK	S	Danmarks Nationalbank (CB)	Finance Inspectorate (MI)[1]
FIN	S	Bank of Finland (CB)	Bank Inspectorate (MF)/Bank of Finland (CB)
F	C	Banque de France (CB)	Banque de France (CB)/ Commission Bancaire[2]
D	S	Deutsche Bundesbank (CB)	Federal Banking Supervisory Office/Deutsche Bundesbank[3]
GR	C	Bank of Greece (CB)	Bank of Greece (CB)
IRL	C	Central Bank of Ireland (CB)	Central Bank of Ireland (CB)
I	C	Banca d'Italia (CB)	Banca d'Italia (CB)
L	S	Bank of Luxembourg (CB)	Commission de Surveillance du Secteur Financier
NL	C	De Nederlandsche Bank (CB)	De Nederlandsche Bank (CB)
P	C	Banco de Portugal (CB)	Banco de Portugal (CB)
S	C	Banco de Espana (CB)	Banco de Espana (CB)
SW	S	Sveriges Riksbank (CB)	Swedish Financial Supervisory Authority
UK	S	Bank of England (CB)	Financial Services Authority[4]
EU	S	European Central Bank (CB)	National authorities
CH	S	Swiss National Bank (CB)	Federal Banking Commission
US	S/C	Federal Reserve Board (CB)	Office of the Comptroller of the Currency (CB)/ Federal Reserve board (CB)/ State Governments/ Federal Deposit Insurance Corp[5]

C = Combined, S = Separated, CB = Central Bank, MF = Ministry of Finance, MI = Ministry of Industry

Notes
1   The Danish Nationalbank is the granter of liquidity support, while the Inspectorate is responsible for the supervision of banks. The Inspectorate has no formal link with the Nationalbank, although there is in practice cooperation between the two on many issues.
2   The Banking Commission (Commission Bancaire) is a composite body chaired by the governor of the Banque de France, with representatives from the Ministry of Finance. The Banking Commission supervises compliance with the prudential regulations. The inspections and on-site examinations are carried out by the Banque de France on behalf of the Banking Commission.
3   The Federal Banking Supervisory Office (Bundesaufsichtsamt für das Kreditwesen) is entrusted with the supervision of banks. It is responsible for sovereign acts, such as licensing and issuing regulations, whereas the Bundesbank is involved in current supervision by collecting and processing bank prudential returns. The Banking Act provides for cooperation between the Supervisory Office and the Bundesbank (i.e.

the two bodies communicate information to each other, and the Supervisory Office has to consult the Bundesbank on new regulations).

4   The Bank of England Bill (October 1997) transferred the banking supervisory responsibilities from the Bank of England to the Financial Services Authority, a single financial supervisor. The Financial Services and Markets Bill (July 1998) integrated all supervisory bodies in one authority.

5   The Office of the Comptroller of the Currency, an agency within the US Treasury Department, supervises national banks and federally licensed branches of foreign banks. The Federal Reserve Board and the State Governments supervise state chartered banks which are members of the Federal Reserve System. State chartered non-member banks are supervised by the State Governments. The Federal Reserve Board has the authority to supervise all bank holding companies and their subsidiaries. In addition, the autonomous Federal Deposit Insurance Corporation has some supervisory responsibilities.

Source: Adapted from Goodhart and Schoenmaker (1995), p. 558.

Table A1.12 *Regulators of banking, securities and insurance in Europe, Japan and the US*

	Banking	Securities	Insurance
B	BS	BS	I
DK	M	M	M
DE	B	S	I
EL	CB	S	I
E	CB	S	I
F	B/CB	S	I
I	CB	S	I
IRL	CB	CB	G
L	BS	BS	I
NL	CB	S	I
AU	G	G	G
P	CB	S	I
SF	BS	BS	I
SW	M	M	M
UK	M	M	M
CH	BS	BS	I
CZ	CB	S	G
H	BS	BS	I
N	M	M	M
PL	CB	S	I
SLOE	CB	S	G
USA	CB	S	I
J	M	M	M

Notes: CB = Central Bank, BS = banking and securities supervisor, M = single financial supervisory authority, B = specialised banking supervisor, S = specialised securities supervisor, I = specialised insurance supervisor, SI = specialised securities and insurance supervisor, G = government department.
Source: Updated and adapted from Goodhart et al. (1997).

Appendix 2   The EU Regulatory Framework for the Free Provision of Financial Services

BANKING

Adopted Legislation and Measures

The basic measures in the area of banking consist of the second banking directive, which defines the modalities for the free provision of banking services across the EU with a single licence (the first banking coordination directive of 1973 instituted the freedom of establishment for banks in the EU) and a series of related directives, such as the own funds directive, which defines the elements that can be considered as own funds, and the solvency ratio directive, which sets the calculation of the capital ratios and the weighting of assets. Other key directives concern the method for consolidated supervision, the limitation of large exposures and the obligatory institution of deposit protection schemes.

- *Second banking directive*: Second Council Directive 89/646 of 17 December 1989 on the coordination of laws, regulations and administrative provisions relating to the taking-up and pursuit of the business of credit institutions and amending directive 77/780/EEC, *OJ* L 386 of 30.12.1989
- *Own funds*: Council Directive 89/299 of 17 April 1989 on the own funds of credit institutions; implementation date 1.1.1993, *OJ* L 124 of 5.5.1989

- *Solvency ratio*: Council Directive 89/647 of 18 December 1989 on a solvency ratio for credit institutions, *OJ* L 386 of 30.12.1989
- *Consolidated supervision*: Council Directive 92/30 of 6 April 1992 on the supervision of credit institutions on a consolidated basis, *OJ* L 110 of 28.4.1992
- *Deposit guarantee scheme*: Directive 94/19/EC of the European Parliament and of the Council of 30 May 1994 on deposit-guarantee schemes, *OJ* L 135 of 31.5.94
- *Large exposures*: Council Directive 92/121 of 21 December 1992 on the monitoring and control of large exposures of credit institutions, *OJ* L 29 of 5.2.1993

Other measures have to do with issues that had to be tackled with the coming into force of a single financial area. They relate to the harmonisation of the annual accounts of banks and the finality of payments.

- *Annual accounts of banks*: Council Directive 86/635 of 8 December 1986 on the annual accounts and consolidated annual accounts for banks and other financial institutions, *OJ* L 372 of 31.12.1986
- *Settlement finality*: Directive 98/26/EC of the European Parliament and of the Council Directive of 19 May 1998 on settlement finality in payment and securities settlement systems, *OJ* L 166 of 11/06/1998

Several directives and recommendations relate to the retail dimension of the single financial market. They set rules on consumer credit, the use of credit cards and the performance of cross-border payments in the EU.

- *Consumer credit*: Council Directive of 22 February 1990 amending directive 87/102/EEC for the approximation of laws, regulations and administrative provisions of the Member States concerning consumer credit, *OJ* L 61 of 10.3.90
- *Credit cards*: Commission Recommendation 87/598 of 8 December 1987 on a European Code of Conduct relating to electronic payment, *OJ* L 365 of 24.12.1987; Commission Recommendation 88/590 of 17 November 1988 concerning payment systems and in particular the relationship between cardholder and card issuers, *OJ* L 317, 24.11.1988
- *Cross-border payments*: Directive 97/5/EC of the European

Parliament and of the Council of 27 January 1997 on cross-border credit transfers, *OJ* L 43 of 14.2.1997

Draft Legislation and Communications

The most important measure awaiting adoption is a draft directive instituting common rules for the winding-up (or failure) of credit institutions. One communication gives guidance on the application of the 'general good' clause in the second banking directive, another deals with consumers and electronic payments.

- *Reorganisation and winding-up of credit institutions*: (amended) Proposal for Council Directive concerning the reorganisation and the winding-up of credit institutions and deposit guarantee schemes COM(85)788 & COM (88)4, *OJ* C 36 of 8.2.1988
- *General good*: Commission Interpretative Communication, Freedom to provide services and the interest of the general good in the second banking directive, *OJ* C 209 of 10.7.1997
- *Electronic payments*: Boosting customers' confidence in electronic means of payment in the single market, Communication from the Commission, COM(97)353 of 09.07.1997

INVESTMENT SERVICES

Adopted Legislation

The basic measure in the domain of investment service is the investment services directive (ISD), which defines the modalities for the free provision of investment services in the EU for brokers and securities markets. The ISD refers to the capital adequacy directive, which sets capital ratios for investment services firms, and for the trading books of banks. The investor compensation schemes directive introduces a minimum level of protection for (retail) clients of investment firms.

- *Investment services (ISD)*: Council Directive 93/6 of 10 May 1993 on investment services in the securities field, *OJ* L 141 of 11 June 1993

- *Capital adequacy (CAD)*: Council Directive 93/22 of 15 March 1993 on the capital adequacy of investment firms and credit institutions, *OJ* L 141 of 11 June 1993; *Value at Risk amendments (CAD II)*: Directive 98/31/EC, *OJ* L 204, 21/07/1998
- *Investor compensation schemes*: Directive 97/7/EC of the Council and the European Parliament on investor compensation schemes, *OJ* L 84 of 26.3.1997

A second series of measures relate to the functioning of capital markets and exchanges, and set minimum rules regarding particulars to be disclosed for stock exchange listings and initial public offerings, to allow for mutual recognition. Other directives make insider trading a statutory offence and require firms to disclose major holdings to the market.

- *Stock exchange admission*: Council directive of 79/279/EEC coordinating the conditions for the admission of securities to official stock exchange listing, *OJ* L 66 of 16.3.1979
- *Stock exchange listing particulars*: Council Directive 87/345 of 22 June 1987 amending Directive 80/390 coordinating the requirement for the drawing-up, scrutiny, and distribution of the listing particulars to be published for the admission of securities to official stock exchange listing, *OJ* L 185 of 4.7.1987; Eurolist amendments, Directive 94/18/EC, *OJ* L 135 of 31.5.1994
- *Mutual recognition of public-offer prospectuses*: Council Directive 90/211 of 23 April 1990 amending directive 80/390 in respect of the mutual recognition of public-offer prospectuses as stock exchange listing particulars, *OJ* L 112 of 3.5.1990
- *Prospectus for public offerings of securities*: Council Directive 89/298 coordinating the requirements for the drawing-up, scrutiny and distribution for the prospectus to be published when securities are offered to the public, *OJ* L 124 of 5.5.1989
- *Regulation of insider trading*: Council Directive 89/592 coordinating regulations on insider trading, *OJ* L 334 of 18.11.1989
- *Publication of information on major holdings*: Council Directive 88/627 on the information to be published when a major holding in a listed company is acquired or disposed of, *OJ* L 348 of 17.12.1988

A final series of measures allow for the cross-border sale of unit trusts or collective investment undertakings in the EU. Two proposed amendments extend the scope of unit trusts and harmonise basic rules for the management of unit trusts.

- *Collective investment undertakings (UCITS)*: Council Directive 85/611 on the coordination of laws relating to undertakings for collective investment in transferable securities, *OJ* L 375 of 31.12.1985; Council Directive 88/220 amending directive 85/611 relating to undertakings for collective investment in transferable securities, *OJ* L 100 of 19.04.1988.

Proposed Legislation

- *UCITS Amendment 2*: Proposal for a European Parliament and Council Directive amending directive 85/611 on the coordination of laws, regulations and administrative provisions relating to undertakings for collective investment in transferable securities (UCITS) with a view to regulating management companies and simplified prospectuses, COM (1998) 451 of 17.07.1998
- *UCITS Amendment 1*: Proposal for a European Parliament and Council Directive amending directive 85/611 on the coordination of laws, regulations and administrative provisions relating to undertakings for collective investment in transferable securities (UCITS), COM(1998) 449 of 17.07.1998

INSURANCE

Adopted Legislation

The free provision of insurance services was instituted in two phases, with limited free provision of services in the second generation directives, and full liberalisation in the third generation directives (the first generation directives instituted freedom of establishment). Regulation is subdivided along the lines of the life and non-life business. A recent measure harmonises the supervision of insurance groups, taking the particularities of risk exposure in insurance groups, as compared to banking, into account.

- *Third non-life insurance directive*: Council Directive 92/49 of 18 June 1992 on the coordination of laws, regulations and administrative provisions relating to direct insurance other than life insurance and amending Directives 73/239/EEC and 88/357/EEC, *OJ* L 228 of 11.8.92

* *Second non-life insurance directive*: Council Directive 88/357 on the coordination of laws, regulations and administrative provisions relating to direct insurance other than life insurance and laying down provisions to facilitate the effective exercise of freedom to provide services and amending directive 73/239, *OJ* L 172 of 4.7.1988
* *Third life insurance directive*: Council Directive 92/96 of 10 November 1992 on the coordination of laws, regulations and administrative provisions relating to life insurance and amending directives 79/267/CEE and 90/619/CEE, *OJ* L 360 of 9.12.92
* *Second life assurance directive*: Council Directive 90/619 on the coordination of laws, regulations and administrative provisions relating to direct life assurance, laying down provisions to facilitate the effective freedom to provide services and amending directive 79/267/EEC, *OJ* L 330 of 29.11.1990
* *Insurance groups*: Directive 98/78/EC of the European Parliament and of the Council of 27 October 1998 on the supplementary supervision of insurance undertakings in an insurance group, *OJ* L 330, 05/12/1998

Special directives were required to harmonise liability in car insurance, to ensure adequate protection of third parties. The role of brokers in the distribution of insurance policies is the subject of another directive. A separate directive was adopted to institute cooperation between insurance supervisors, which, in banking, is part of the first banking coordination directive.

* *Car insurance:* Council Directive 90/618 amending, particularly as regards motor vehicle liability insurance, Directive 73/239/EEC and Directive 88/357/EEC which concern the coordination of laws, regulations and administrative provisions relating to the direct insurance other than life assurance, *OJ* L 330 of 29.11.1990.
* *Motor vehicle liability insurance—passengers' coverage*: Third Council Directive 90/232 on the approximation of laws of the member states relating to insurance against civil liability in respect of the use of motor vehicles, *OJ* L 129 of 19.5.1990
* *Intermediaries*: Council Directive of 13 December 1976 on measures to facilitate the effective exercise of freedom of establishment and freedom to provide services in respect of the activities of insurance agents and brokers and, in particular, transitional measures

in respect of those activities, *OJ* L 26 of 31.01.1977; Commission recommendation of 18 December 1991 on insurance intermediaries, *OJ* L 19 of 28.1.92

- *Annual accounts of insurance companies*: Council Directive 91/674 on the annual and consolidated accounts of insurance undertakings, *OJ* L 374 of 19.12.1991
- *Insurance Committee*: Council Directive 91/675 setting up an Insurance Committee, *OJ* L 374 of 19.12.1991

Draft Legislation and Communications

As in banking, the most important draft piece of legislation concerns the harmonisation of winding-up procedures. A new proposal is awaited covering the freedom of management and investment of pension funds, on which an earlier proposal was withdrawn. A draft communication is being debated regarding the application of 'general good' in the insurance sector.

- *Winding-up of insurance companies*: Amended proposal for Council Directive on the coordination of laws, regulations and administrative provisions relating to the compulsory winding-up of direct insurance undertakings, COM(86)768 and COM(89)394
- *Fourth motor insurance directive*: Proposal for a European Parliament and Council Directive on the approximation of laws of the member states relating to insurance against civil liability in respect of the use of motor vehicles and amending directives 73/239/EEC and 92/49/EEC, COM(97)510 of 10.10.1997
- *Pension funds*: Commission communication on the freedom of management and investment of funds held by institutions for retirement provision, C 360/08, *OJ* C 360 of 17.12.94; (Proposal for a Council Directive relating to the freedom of management and investment of funds held by institutions of retirement provision, COM(91)301, *OJ* C 312 of 3.12.1991, amended proposal COM(93)237 of 26 May 1993, withdrawn on 7 December 1994.) Supplementary pensions in the Single Market, a Green Paper, COM(97)283 of 10.06.1997
- *General good*: Draft Commission Interpretative Communication, Freedom to provide services and the interest of the general good in the sector of insurance, SEC(97)1824 of 10.10.1997

HORIZONTAL MEASURES AND COMMUNICATIONS

Three directives are of a 'horizontal' nature and apply to the financial services sector as a whole. There is first the 1988 directive defining the freedom of capital movements, which at the same time signalled the start of Phase 1 of EMU. The money laundering directive requires financial institutions to inform authorities about suspected transactions and obliges them to ask for identification of clients depositing or investing significant amounts of money. The BCCI directive was adopted as a result of the failure of the BCCI bank and reinforces certain elements of prudential supervision, such as the exchange of information between auditors and supervisors. A new proposal on the distance selling of financial services is currently being debated.

- *Freedom of capital movements*: Council Directive 88/361 of 24 June 1988 for the implementation of Article 67 of the Treaty, *OJ* L 178 of 08.07.1988
- *Money laundering*: Council Directive 91/308 of 10 June 1991 on the prevention of the use of the financial system for the purpose of money laundering, *OJ* L 166 of 28.6.91
- *BCCI follow-up directive*: European Parliament and Council Directive amending Directives 77/780/EEC and 89/646/EEC in the field of credit institutions, Directives 73/239/EEC and 92/49/EEC in the field of non-life insurance, Directives 79/267/EEC and 92/96/EEC in the field of life assurance, Directive 93/22/EEC in the field of investment firms, and Directive 85/611 in the field of undertakings for collective investment in transferable securities (UCITS), with a view to reinforcing prudential supervision, *OJ* L 168 of 18.7.95
- *Distance selling of financial services (draft)*: Proposal for a directive of the European Parliament and the Council concerning the distance marketing of consumer financial services, COM(98)0468, *OJ* C 385 of 11.12.1998

Two horizontal communications address consumer issues in the financial sector and the adaptation of the regulatory framework for financial services to EMU.

- *Consumer issues*: Financial Services: Enhancing Consumer Confidence, Communication from the European Commission, COM(97)309 of 26.06.1997

- *Financial Services Action Plan*: Implementing the framework for financial markets, COM(1999)232 of 11.05.99

EURO LEGISLATION

The legal framework for the introduction of the euro and issues relating to the transition phase 1999–2002 are addressed in two directives. The first one affects all EU countries, the second concerns the participating member states in EMU.

- *Art. 235 Regulation*: Council Regulation (EC) No. 1103/97 of 17 June 1997 on certain provisions relating to the introduction of the euro, *OJ* L 162, 19/06/1997
- *Art. 109L(4) Regulation*: Council Regulation No. 974/98 of 3 May 1998 on the introduction of the euro, *OJ* L 139 of 11.05.98

Table A2.1 *The regulatory framework for free provision of financial services in the EU*

	Banking	Investment services	Non-life insurance	Life insurance
Key directives	Second banking directive	Investment services directive (ISD)	Third non-life insurance directive	Third life insurance directive
	Own funds directive	Capital adequacy directive (CAD)	Second non-life insurance directive	Second life insurance directive
	Solvency ratios directive or CAD for trading book	Value at risk models (CAD II)		[pension funds]
		Unit trusts (UCITS)		
Consolidation	Consolidated supervision		Supervision of insurance groups	
Supplementary directives	Deposit insurance directive	Investor compensation schemes	Car liability insurance	
	Large exposures directive			
Other measures	Money laundering directive	Insider trading	Insurance intermediaries	
	Settlement finality	Major holdings		
	Cross-border payments	Public offer prospectus		
	Consumer credit	Listing particulars		
Annual accounts	Annual accounts of banks		Annual accounts of insurance companies	
Cooperation between supervisors	Banking advisory committee	[Securities committee]	Insurance committee	
		BCCI follow-up directive		
Winding-up	of banks*		of insurance companies*	

* Not yet adopted, as at July 1999.

REFERENCES

Aglietta, Michel and de Boissieu, Christian (1998). Problèmes pruden-tiels. In *Coordination européenne des politiques economiques*. Conseil d'Analyse Économique, Paris.

Alworth, J.S. and Borio, C.E.V. (1993). *Commercial Paper Markets: A Survey*. BIS Economic Papers, No. 37, April. Bank for International Settlements, Basel.

Arnold, Ivo (1998). The third leg stool, Financial Stability as a tool for EMU. Mimeo.

Bank for International Settlements (1998). *International Banking and Financial Market Developments*. November, Basel.

Bank of England (1998). *Practical Issues Arising from the Introduction of the Euro*. Various issues.

Becht, Marco (1997). *Strong Blockholders, Weak Owners and the Need for European Mandatory Disclosure*. European Corporate Governance Network, Executive Report, October.

Beltratti, Andrea (1999). *The Effect of the Euro on Asset Allocation and European Investors*. CEPS Research Report. Centre for European Policy Studies, Brussels.

Benzie, Richard (1992). *The Development of the International Bond Market*. BIS Economic Papers, No. 32, January. Bank for International Settlements, Basel.

Bini-Smaghi, Lorenzo (1998). Who takes care of financial stability. Mimeo.

Bishop, Graham (1991). *The EC's Public Debt Disease: Discipline with Credit Spreads and Cure with Price Stability*. Salomon Brothers, May.

Bishop, Graham (1998). Securitising European Savings, Delivering the benefits of EMU. Salomon Smith Barney, December.

Borio, Claudio (1995). The Structure of Credit to the Non-government Sector and the Transmission Mechanism of Monetary Policy: A Cross-country Comparison. BIS, Basel.

Brookes, Martin (1998). Winners and Losers in the Euro Bond Market. Goldman Sachs, *European Weekly Analyst*, 30 January.

Brookes, Martin and Winkelmann, Kurt (1998). *Government Bond Markets in EMU*. Goldman Sachs, March.

Cecchini, Paolo (1988). The European Challenge 1992. Commission of the EC.

Clifford Chance (1997). *The Reform of the UK Financial Regulatory System*. August.

Clifford Chance (1998). *The Draft Financial Services and Markets Bill. A Framework for the Future*. September.

Comité Européen des Assurances (CEA), Annual Statistics. Various issues.

Crockett, Andrew (1997). *The Theory and Practice of Financial Stability.* Essays in International Finance, No. 203, Princeton University, NJ.

Dale, Richard, and Wolfe, Simon (1998). The Structure of Financial Regulation. *Journal of Financial Regulation and Compliance*, **6**(4) 326–350.

Danthine, Jean-Pierre, Giavazzi, Francesco, Vives, Xavier and von Thadden, Ernst-Ludwig (1999). *The Future of European Banking. Monitoring European Integration.* CEPR, Centre for Economic Policy Research, London.

Dassesse, Marc (1997). A Courageous Initiative and an Important Precedent: The Commission's Interpretative Communication on the Second Banking Directive. *Butterworths Journal of International Banking and Financial Law*, **12**(8), September.

Daveri, Francesco and Tabellini, Guido (1997). *Unemployment, Growth and Taxation in Industrial Countries.* CEPR Discussion Paper 1681.

Davis, Stephen and Lannoo, Karel (1998). Shareholder Voting in Europe. CEPS, Mimeo.

De Bandt, Olivier (1998). EMU and the Structure of the European Banking System. Paper presented at the Suerf Conference, October.

Dermine, Jean and Hillion, Pierre (eds) (1999). *European Capital Markets with a Single Currency.* Oxford: Oxford University Press.

De Ryck, Koen (1996). *European Pension Funds: Their Impact on Capital Markets and Competitiveness.* European Federation for Retirement Provision (EFRP).

Deutsche Bank Research (1996). EMU and Financial Markets—Some Issues and Prospects. *EMU Watch*, No. 22, December.

Dornbusch, Rudiger, Favero, Carlo and Giavazzi, Francesco (1998). *A Red Letter Day?* CEPR Discussion Paper No. 1804, Centre for Economic Policy Research, London, February.

Eichengreen, Barry (1992). Designing a Central Bank for Europe: A Cautionary Tale from the Early Years of the Federal Reserve System. In Matthew Canzoneri, Vittorio Grilli and Paul Mason (eds), *Establishing a Central Bank: Issues in Europe and Lessons from the US.* Cambridge: Cambridge University Press, pp. 13–48.

Enoch, Charles, Stella, Peter and Khamis, May (1997). Transparency and Ambiguity in Central Bank Safety Net Operations. IMF working paper 97/138, October.

European Central Bank (1998). The Single Monetary Policy in Stage Three: General Documentation on ESCB Monetary Policy Instruments and Procedures. Frankfurt, September.

European Central Bank (1999). Possible Effects of EMU on the EU Banking System in the Medium to Long Term. Frankfurt, February.

European Commission (1995a). *Accounting Harmonisation: A New Strategy vis-à-vis International Harmonisation.* COM(95)508. Brussels.

European Commission (1995b). The Simplification of the Operating Regulations for Public Limited Companies in the EU. Brussels, December.

European Commission (1997a). External Aspects of EMU. Commission Staff Working Document. Brussels.

European Commission (1997b). *Supplementary Pensions in the Single Market. A Green Paper.* Brussels.

European Commission (1997c). *The Single Market Review: Credit Institutions and Banking,* Vol. II, 3. Kogan Page: London.

European Commission (1997d). *The Single Market Review: Intra-EU Multi-Currency Management Costs,* Vol. III, 6. Kogan Page: London.

European Commission (1997e). *The Impact of the Introduction of the Euro on Capital Markets* (Giovannini Group). COM (97) 337 of 2 July 1997. Brussels.

European Commission (1998a). *Debt Redenomination and Market Convention in Stage III of EMU.* Euro Papers, No. 28, July 1998. Brussels.

European Commission (1998b). *Financial Services: Building a Framework for Action.* Communication to the Council and the European Parliament, 28 October. Brussels.

European Commission (1999). *Financial Services Action Plan.* May.

European Federation of Investment Funds (FEFSI). *Annual Statistics,* various years. Brussels.

European Monetary Institute (1997a). The Single Monetary Policy in Stage III of EMU—Specification of the Operational Framework. January.

European Monetary Institute (1997b). The Single Monetary Policy in Stage III—General documentation on ESCB monetary policy instruments and procedures. September.

European Mortgage Federation (1998). *Hypostat 1987–1997.*

European Shadow Financial Regulatory Committee (1998). EMU, the ECB and Financial Supervision. Statement No. 2, 19 October.

Federation of Stock Exchanges in the EC (1993). *Share Ownership Structure in Europe.*

Federation of Stock Exchanges in the EC (1990). *Off-Exchange Trading.*

Federation of European Stock Exchanges (FESE). *European Stock Exchange Statistics. Annual Report,* various issues.

Fédération Internationale des Bourses de Valeurs (FIBV) Annual Statistics, various years.

FEE (1997). *Conceptual Accounting Frameworks in Europe*. May.

Fender, Ingo and von Hagen, Jurgen (1998). Central Bank Policy in a More Perfect Financial System. ZEI policy paper B98–03.

Folkerts-Landau, David and Garber, Peter (1992). The ECB: A Bank or a Monetary Policy Rule. In Matthew Canzoneri, Vittorio Grilli and Paul Mason (eds), *Establishing a Central Bank: Issues in Europe and Lessons from the US*. Cambridge: Cambridge University Press.

French, Kenneth and Poterba, James (1991). Investor Diversification and International Equity Markets. *American Economic Review*, May, 222–226.

Friedman, Milton and Schwartz, Anna Jacobson (1963). *A Monetary History of the United States, 1867–1960*. Princeton NJ: Princeton University Press.

Gerlach, Stefan and Smets, Frank (1995). *The Monetary Transmission Mechanism: Evidence from the G-7 Countries*. BIS Working Paper No. 26, Bank for International Settlements, Basel.

Giddy, Ian, Saunders, Anthony and Walter, Ingo (1996). Clearance and Settlement. In Benn Steil (ed.), *The European Equity Markets*. ECMI, London.

Goodhart, Charles, Hartmann, Philipp, Llewellyn, David T., Rojas-Suarez, Liliana and Weisbrod, Steven R. (1997). *Financial Regulation: Why, How and Where Now?* Routledge: London.

Goodhart, Charles and Schoenmaker, Dirk (1995). Should the Functions of Monetary Policy and Banking Supervision be Separated? *Oxford Economic Papers*, **47**, 539–560.

Gros, Daniel (1998a). Macroeconomic Policy in the First Year of Euroland. 1st Annual Report of the CEPS Macroeconomic Policy Group, Brussels, December.

Gros, Daniel (1998b). European Financial Markets and Global Financial Turmoil: Any Danger of a Credit Crunch? CEPS working document No. 127, Brussels.

Gros, Daniel and Lannoo, Karel (1996). *The Passage to the Euro*. CEPS Working Party Report No. 15, Centre for European Policy Studies, Brussels.

Gros, Daniel and Thygesen, Niels (1998c). *The European Monetary System*, Longman: London.

Group of Thirty (1997). *Global Institutions, National Supervision and Systemic Risk*. A Study Group Report.

Hartmann, Philip (1996). *The Future of the Euro as an International Currency: A Transactions Perspective*. CEPS Research Report No. 20, Centre for European Policy Studies, Brussels.

International Monetary Fund (1998). *International Capital Markets, Developments, Prospects and Key Policy Issues.* September.

International Securities Markets Association (ISMA) (1997). *The Repo Market in Euro: Making It Work.*

Kaufman, George G. (1995). Comment on Systemic Risk. *Research in Financial Services Private and Public Policy,* **7**, 47–52.

Kaufman, George G. (1996). Bank Failures, Systemic Risk and Regulation. *Cato Journal,* **16**(1), 17–45.

Lannoo, Karel (1995). *Corporate Governance in Europe.* CEPS Working Party Report No. 12, Centre for European Policy Studies, Brussels.

Lannoo, Karel (1996). The Draft Pension Funds Directive and the Financing of Pensions in the EU. *The Geneva Papers for Risk and Insurance,* **21**(78), January.

Lannoo, Karel (1998). *From 1992 to EMU: The Implications for Prudential Supervision.* CEPS Research Report No. 23, Centre for European Policy Studies, Brussels, June.

Lannoo, Karel (1999). A European Perspective on Corporate Governance. *Journal of Common Market Studies,* **37**(2), June.

Lee, Ruben (1998). *What is an Exchange? The Automation, Management and Regulation of Financial Markets.* Oxford: Oxford University Press.

Masson, Paul R. and Turtelboom, Bart G. (1997). *Characteristics of the Euro, the Demand for Reserves and Policy Coordination under EMU.* IMF Working Paper, April.

Merrill Lynch (1999). European Fixed Income Strategy, 1999—The Year Ahead. January.

McCauley, Robert N. and White, William (1997). The Euro and European Financial Markets. Paper presented at the IMF seminar on EMU and the International Monetary System.

Molyneux, Philip, Gardener, Edward and Van der Vennet, Rudi (1997). *The Strategic Implications of EMU for Banks.* CEPS Business Policy Report No. 4, Centre for European Policy Studies, Brussels.

Molyneux, Philip (1997). Internet and the Global Challenges for Financial Services in Europe. Paper presented at a CEPS seminar, Brussels, October.

Monticelli, Carlo and Papi, Ugo (1996). *European Integration, Monetary Coordination, and the Demand for Money.* Oxford: Oxford University Press.

OECD (1998). *Banking Profitability Statistics.*

OECD (1997). *Institutional Investors.* Statistical Yearbook.

Padoa-Schioppa, Tommaso (1999). Banking Supervision in EMU. Speech at the London School of Economics, London, 24 February.

Padoa-Schioppa, Tommaso (1996). 'Developments in the Field of Banking Supervision', Address to the 9th International Conference of Banking Supervisors, Stockholm, 12–14 June.

Pagano, Marco (1998). The Changing Microstructure of European Equity Markets. In Guido Ferrarini, *European Securities Markets, The Investment Services Directive and Beyond*. Dordrecht: Kluwer.

Prati, Alessandro and Schinasi, Garry (1998). Will the ECB be the Lender of Last Resort in EMU? Paper presented at the SUERF Conference, Frankfurt, October.

Price Waterhouse (1997). *Corporate Taxes, A Worldwide Summary*, London.

Problèmes économiques (1997). *Le système financier international*, No. 2541/2542, November, La documentation française.

Salomon Brothers (1997). *World Bond Markets*, September.

Salomon Smith Basney (1999). *World Bond Markets*, July.

Schinasi, Garry J. (1997). *European Monetary Union and International Capital Markets: Structural Implications and Risks*. IMF Working Paper, WP/97/62, May 1997.

Schoenmaker, Dirk (1995). Banking Supervision in Stage III of EMU. In *The Single Market in Banking: From 1992 to EMU*. CEPS Research Report No. 17, Centre for European Policy Studies, Brussels.

Steil, Benn (1998). Regional Financial Market Integration, Learning from the European Experience. Royal Institute for International Affairs, London, April.

Steil, Benn (ed.) (1996). *The European Equity Markets*. ECMI, London.

Steinherr, Alfred (1998). *Derivatives, the Wild Beast of Finance*. Chichester: Wiley.

Steinherr, Alfred (1999). European Futures and Options Markets in a Single Currency Environment. In Jean Dermine and Pierre Hillion (eds), *European Capital Markets with a Single Currency*. Oxford.

Taylor, Michael (1995). *'Twin Peaks': A Regulatory Structure for the New Century*. Centre for the Study of Financial Innovation, No. 20, December.

Tesar, Linda and Werner, Ingrid (1995). Home Bias and High Turnover. *Journal of International Money and Finance*, **14**(4), August, 467–492.

Van der Vennet, Rudi (1998). Cost and Profit Dynamics in Financial Conglomerates and Universal Banks. Paper presented at the Suerf Conference, October.

von Hagen, Jürgen (1997). Monetary Policy and Institutions in the EMU. *Swedish Economic Policy Journal*, **4**(1), Spring.

Walter, Ingo (1998a). Globalisation of Markets and Financial Center Competition. INSEAD working paper, 98/30.

Walter, Ingo (1998b). The Global Asset Management Industry: Competitive Structure, Conduct and Performance. INSEAD working paper 98/36.

White, William R. (1998). *The Coming Transformation of Continental European Banking.* BIS Working Papers No. 54, June. Bank for International Settlements, Basel.

Wouters, Jan (1997). Conflicts of Laws and the Single Market for Financial Services. *Maastricht Journal of European and Comparative Law,* **4**(3).

Index